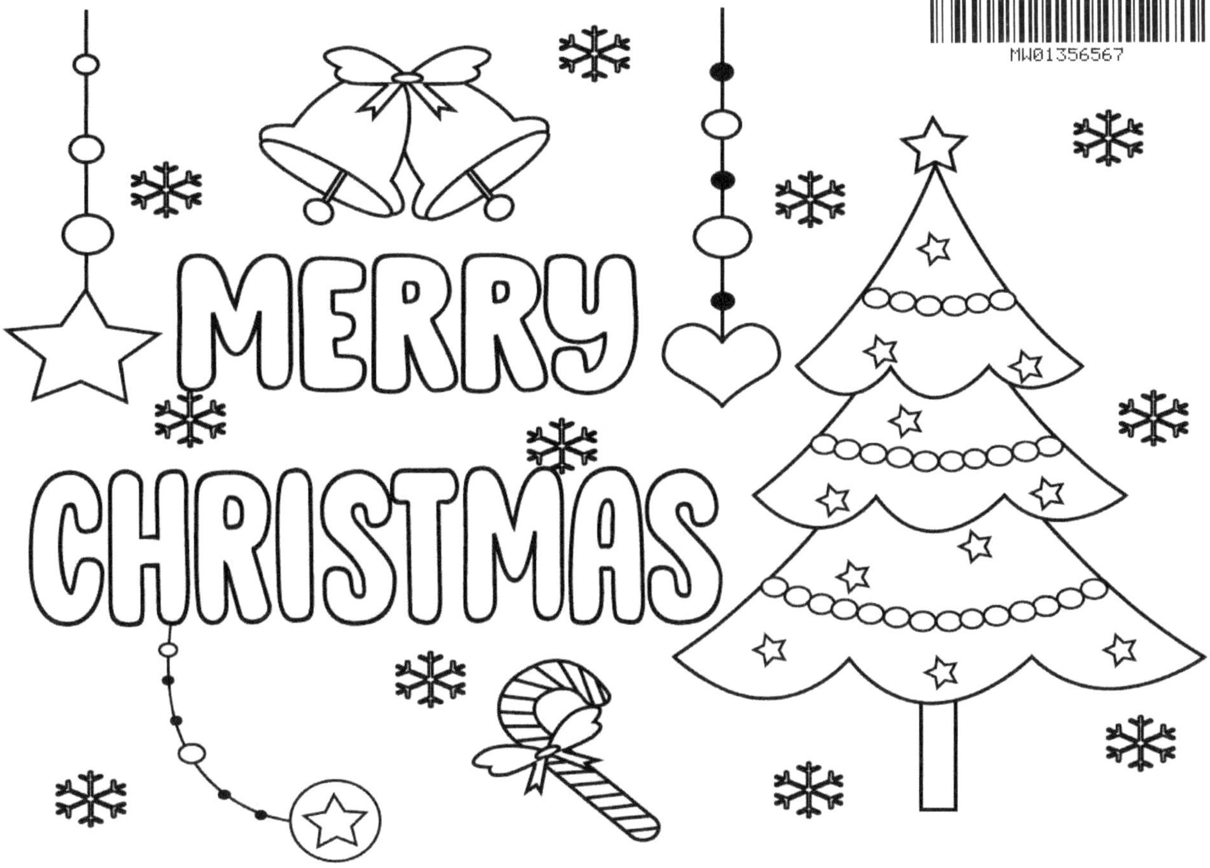

This Book Belongs To...

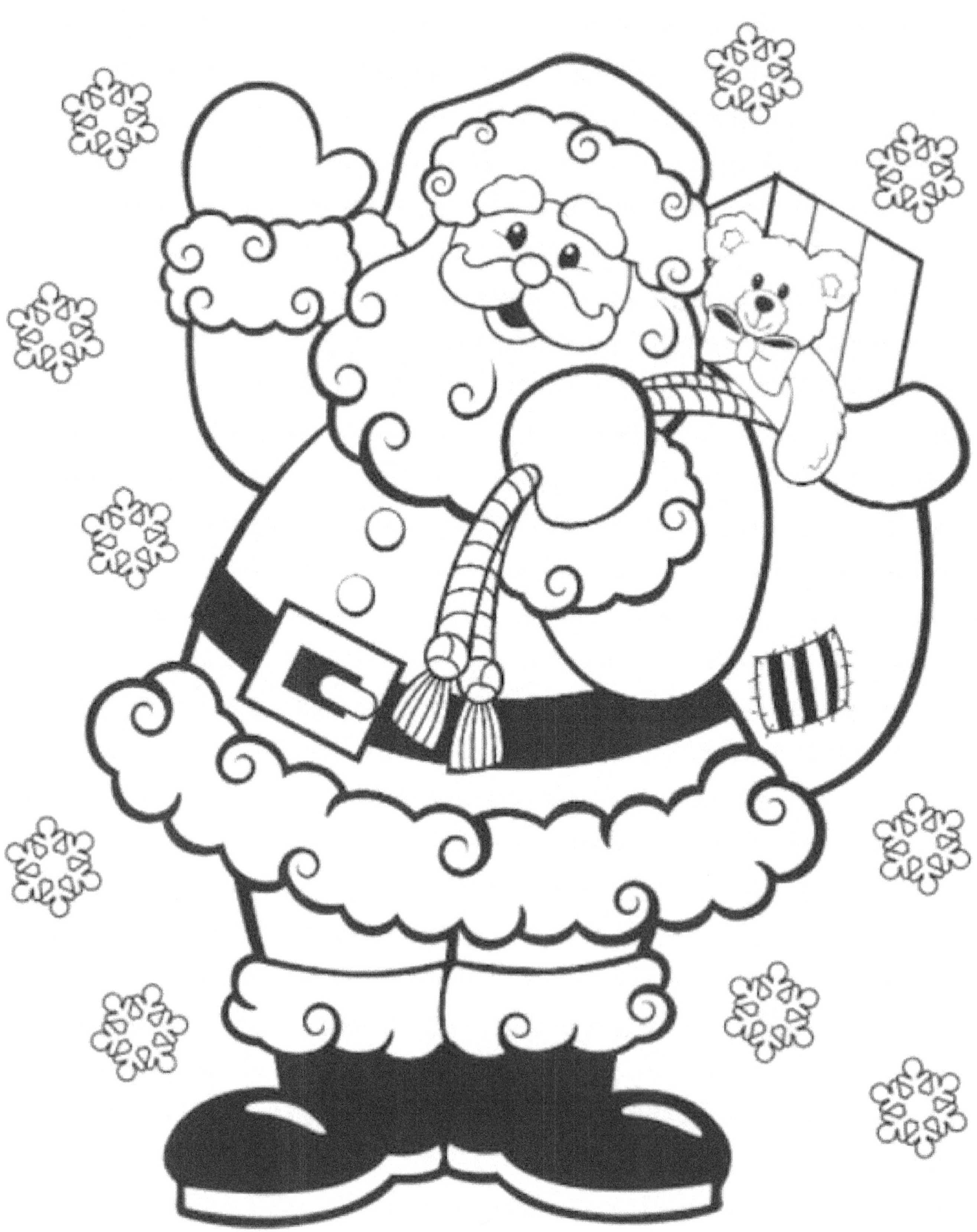

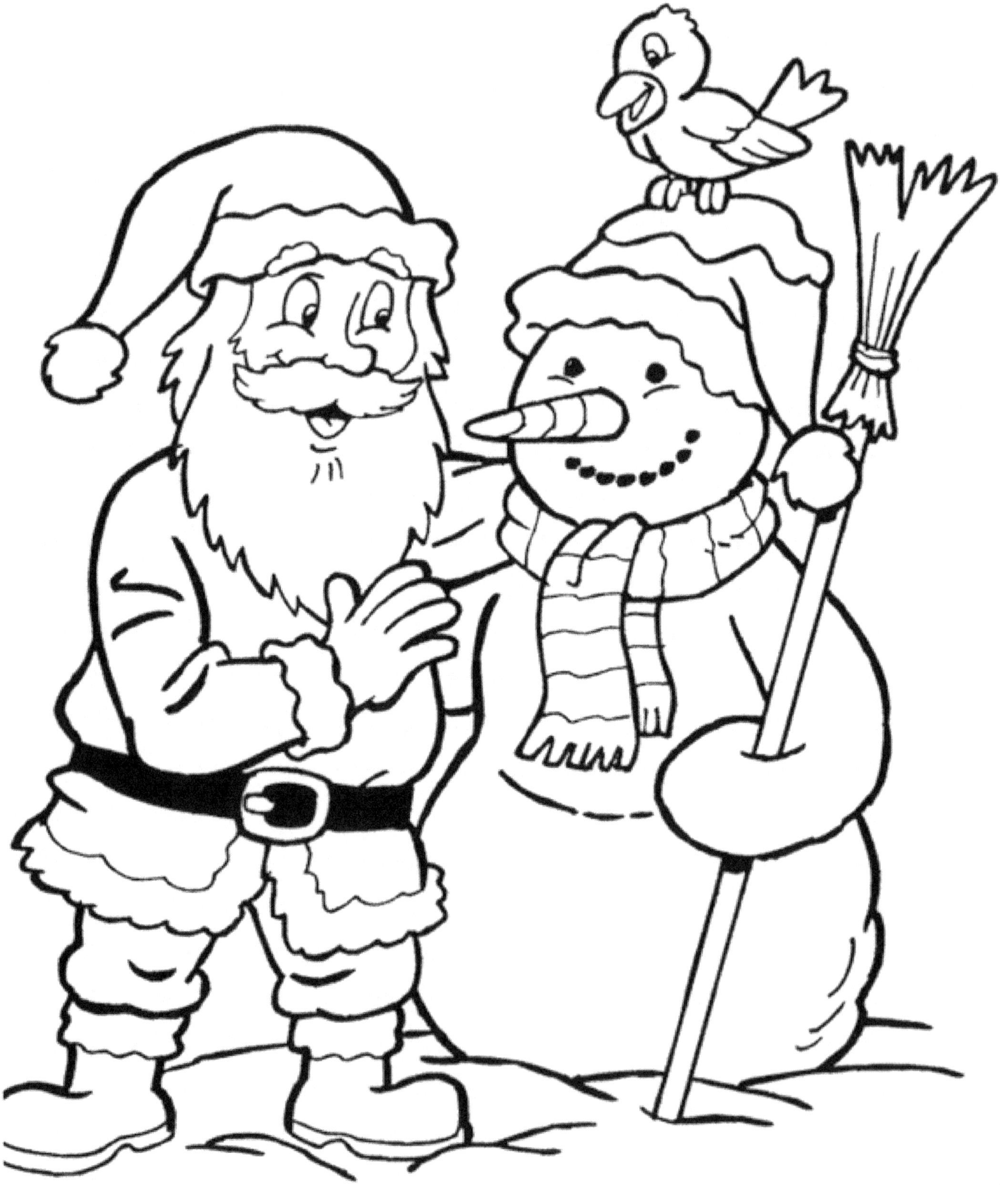

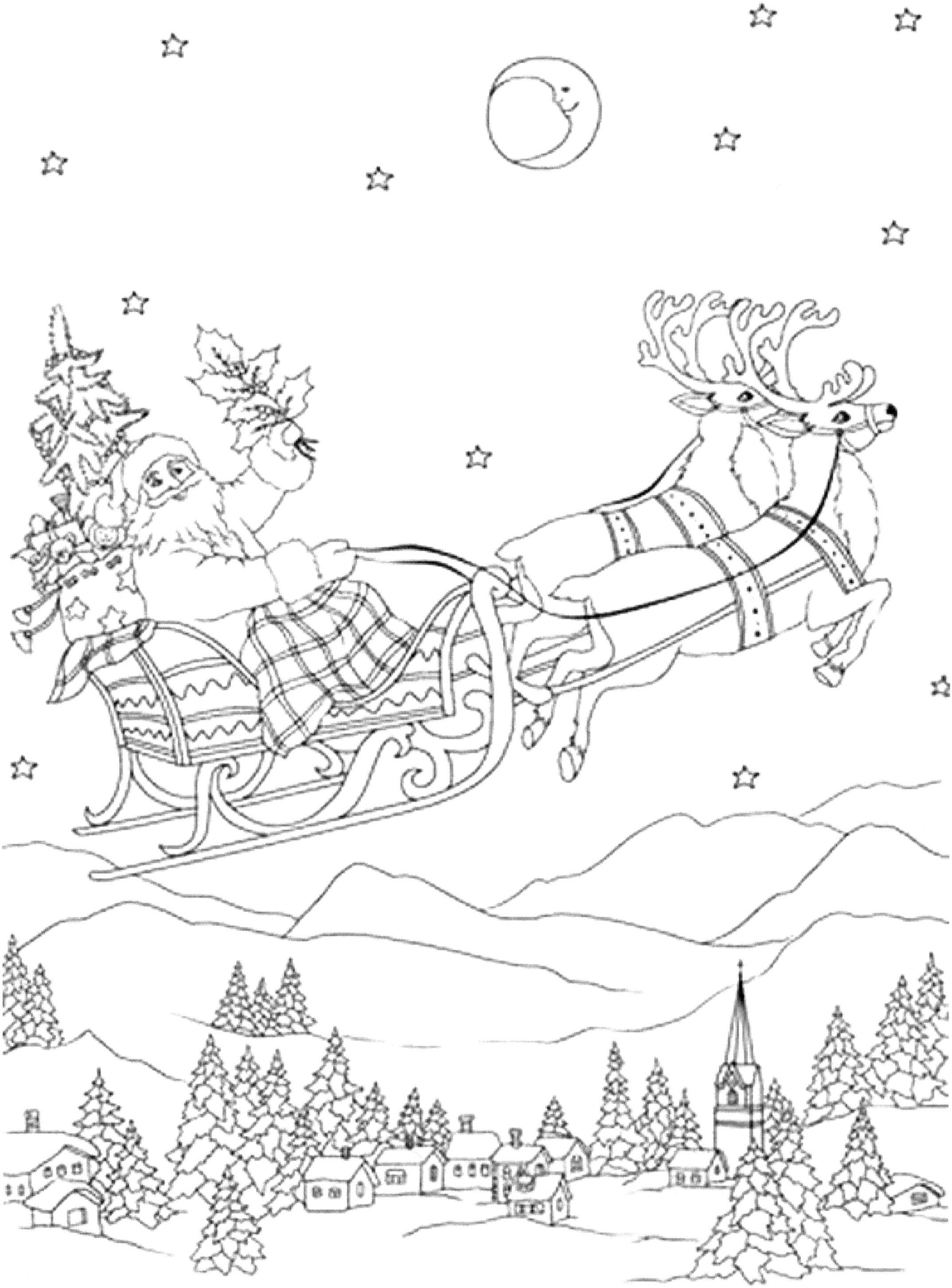

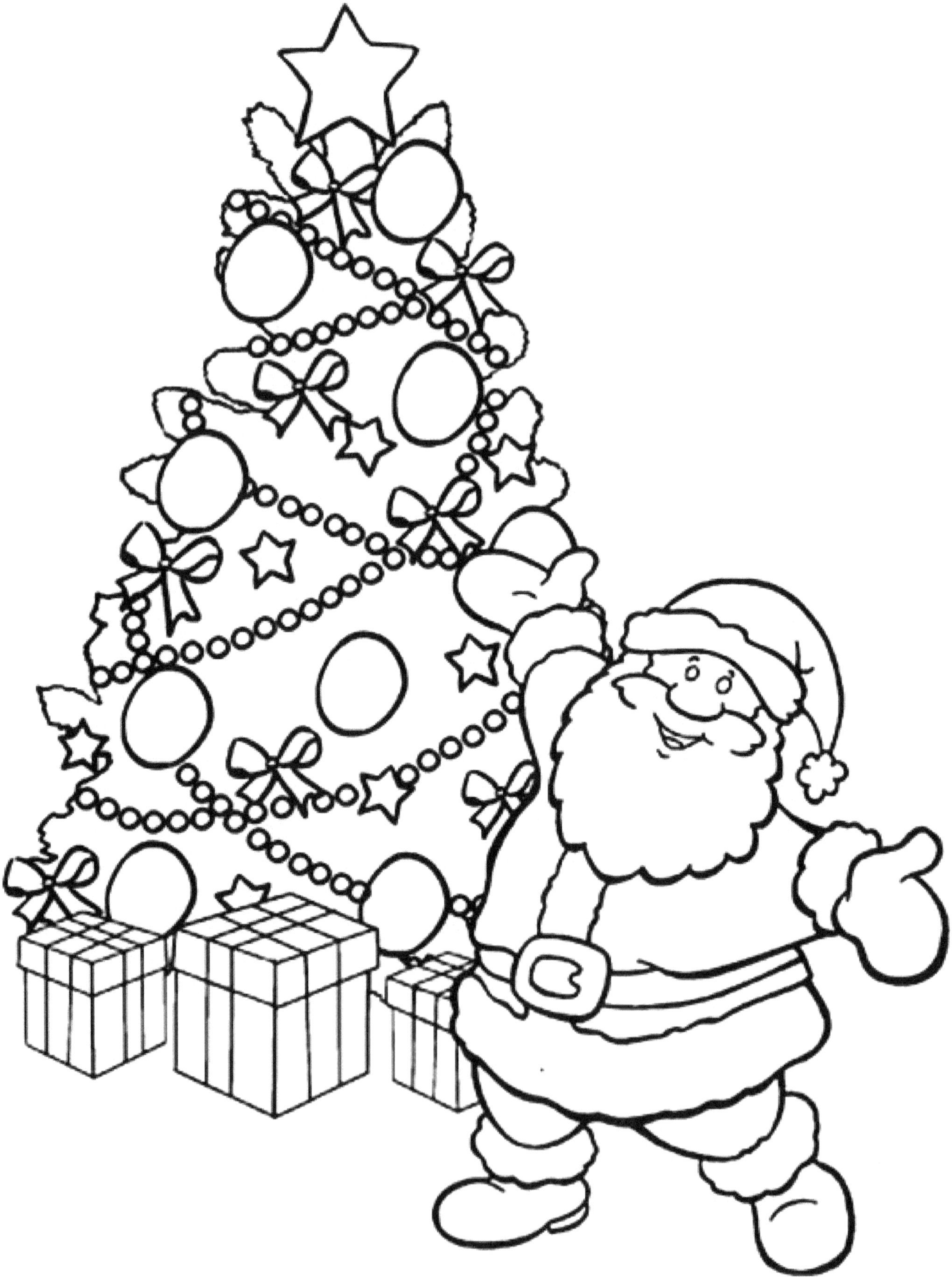

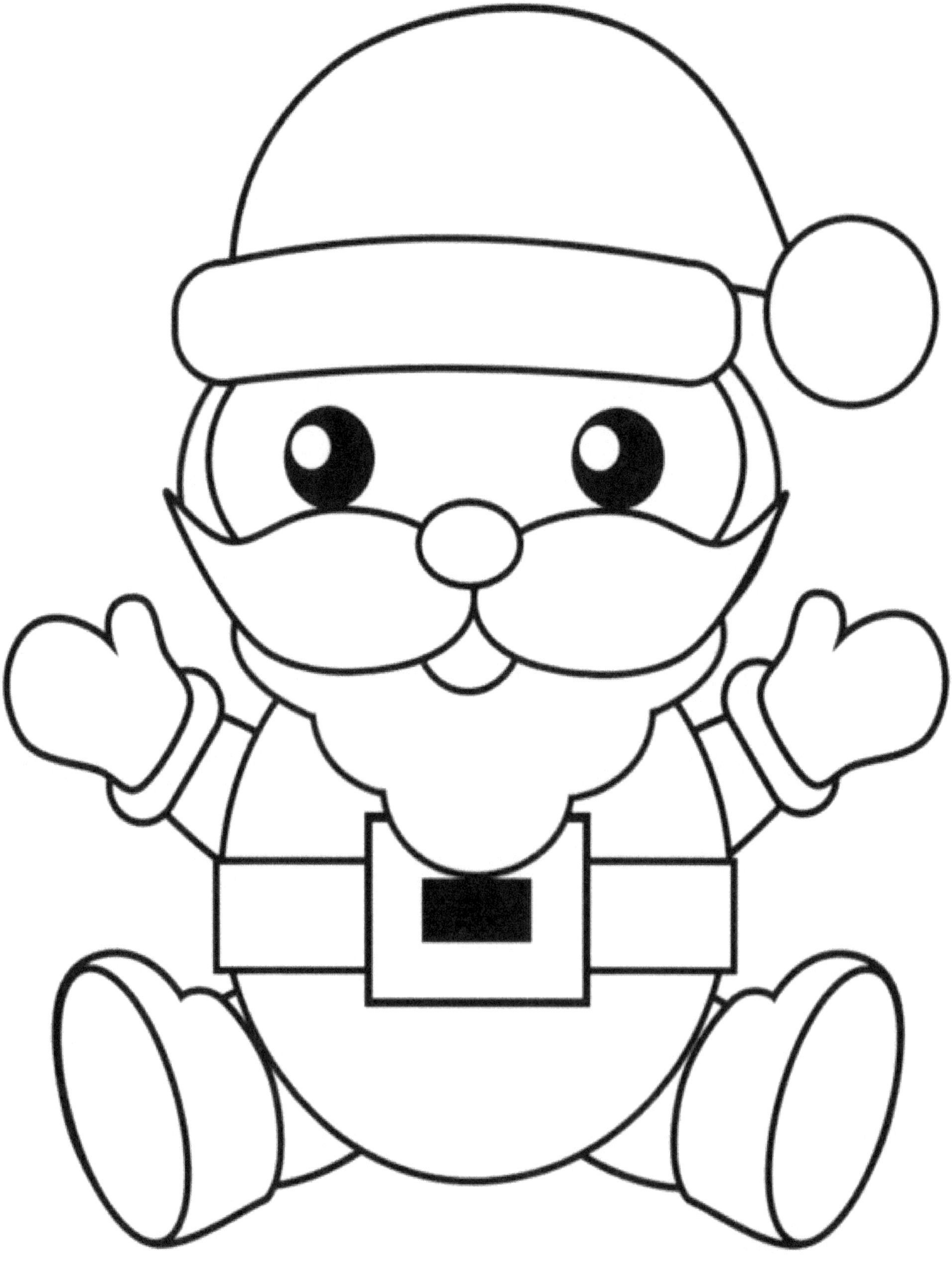

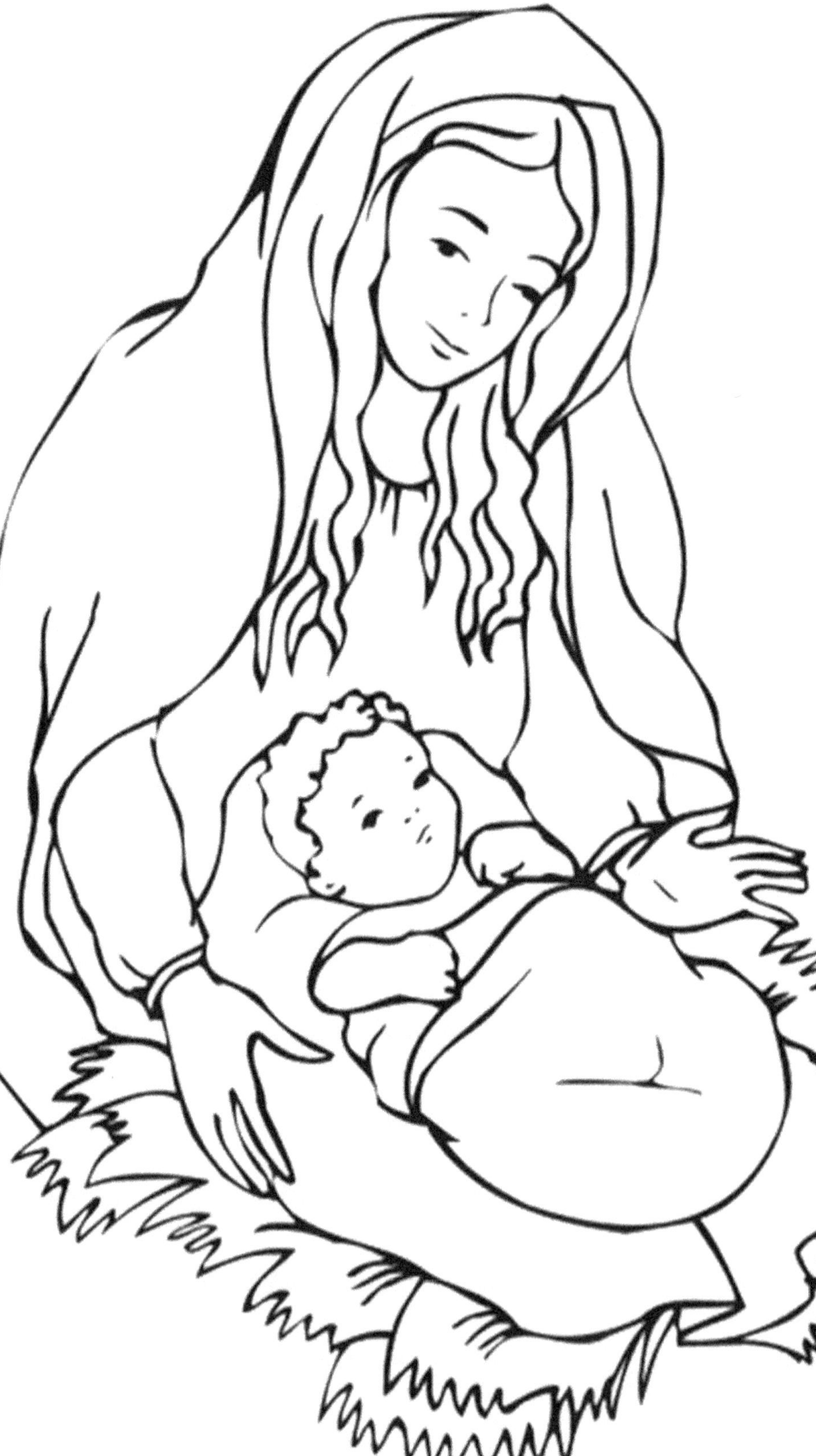

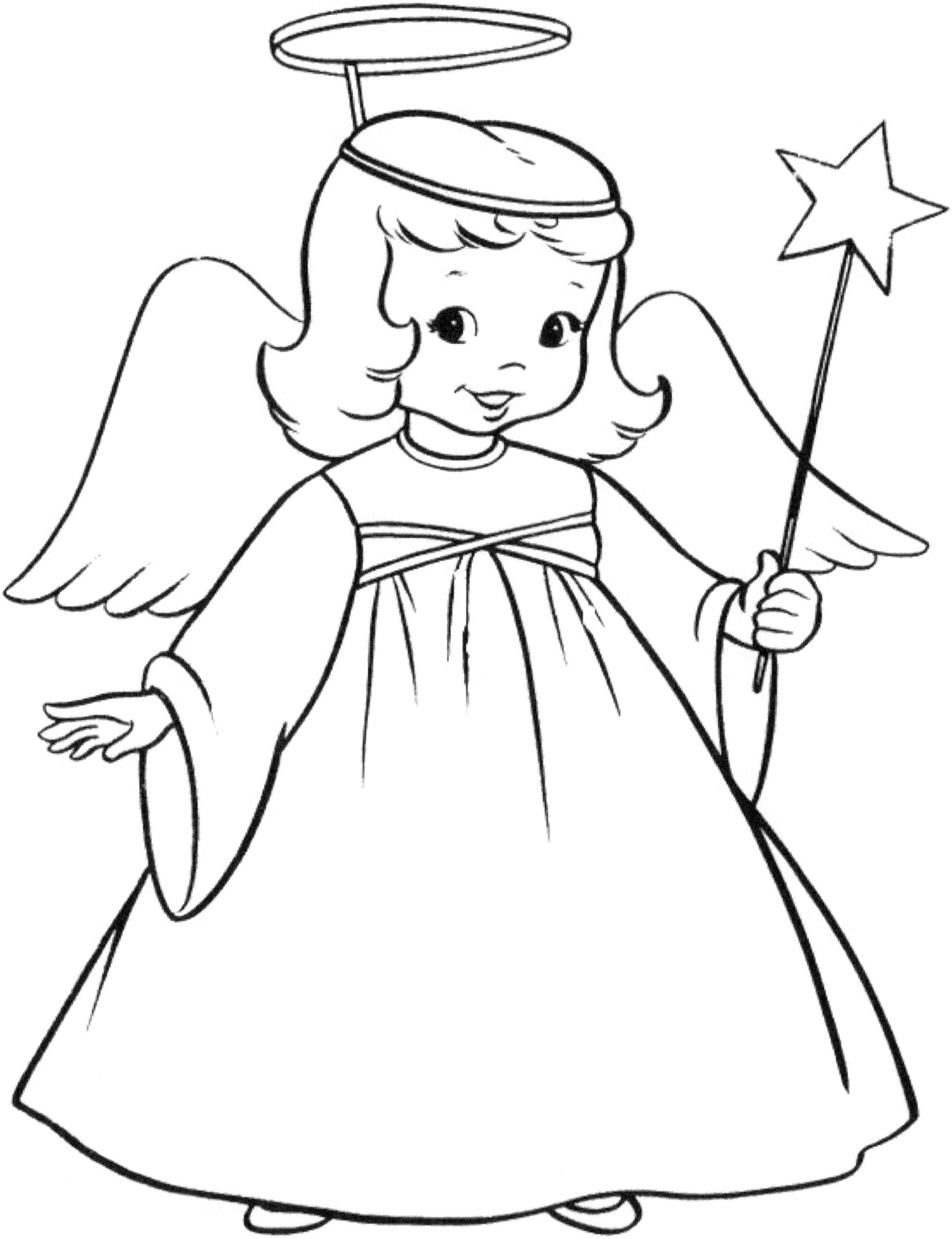

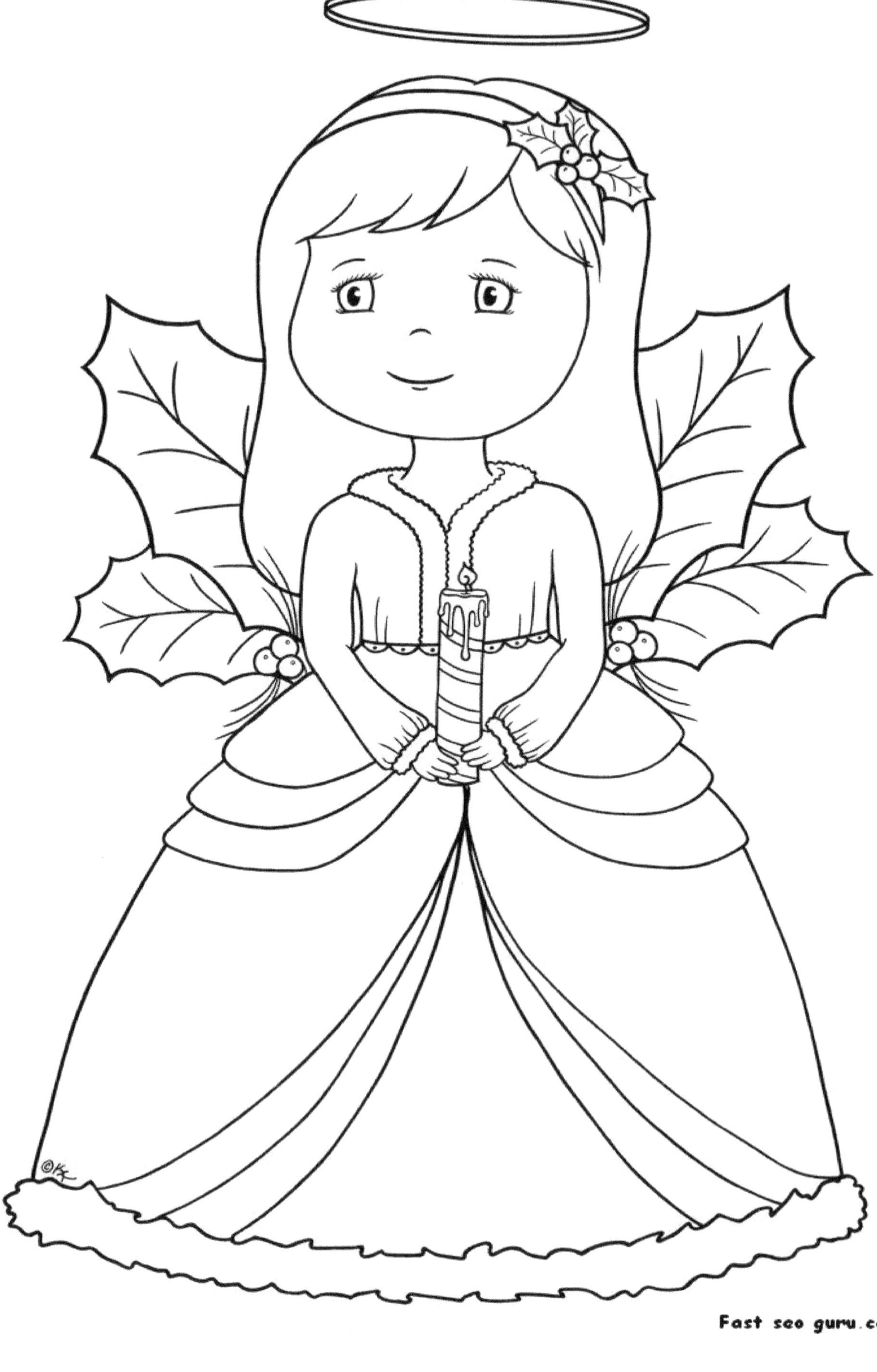

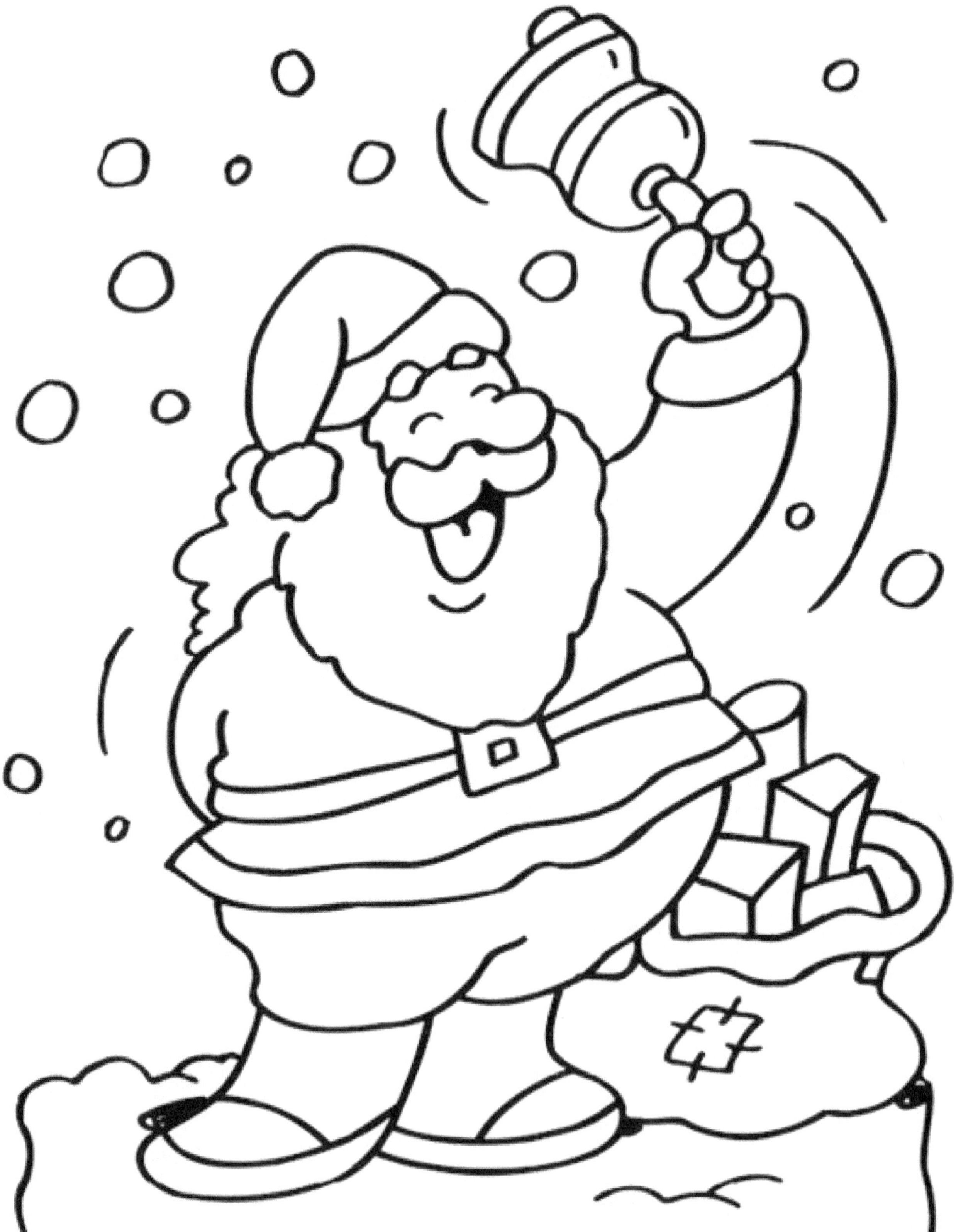

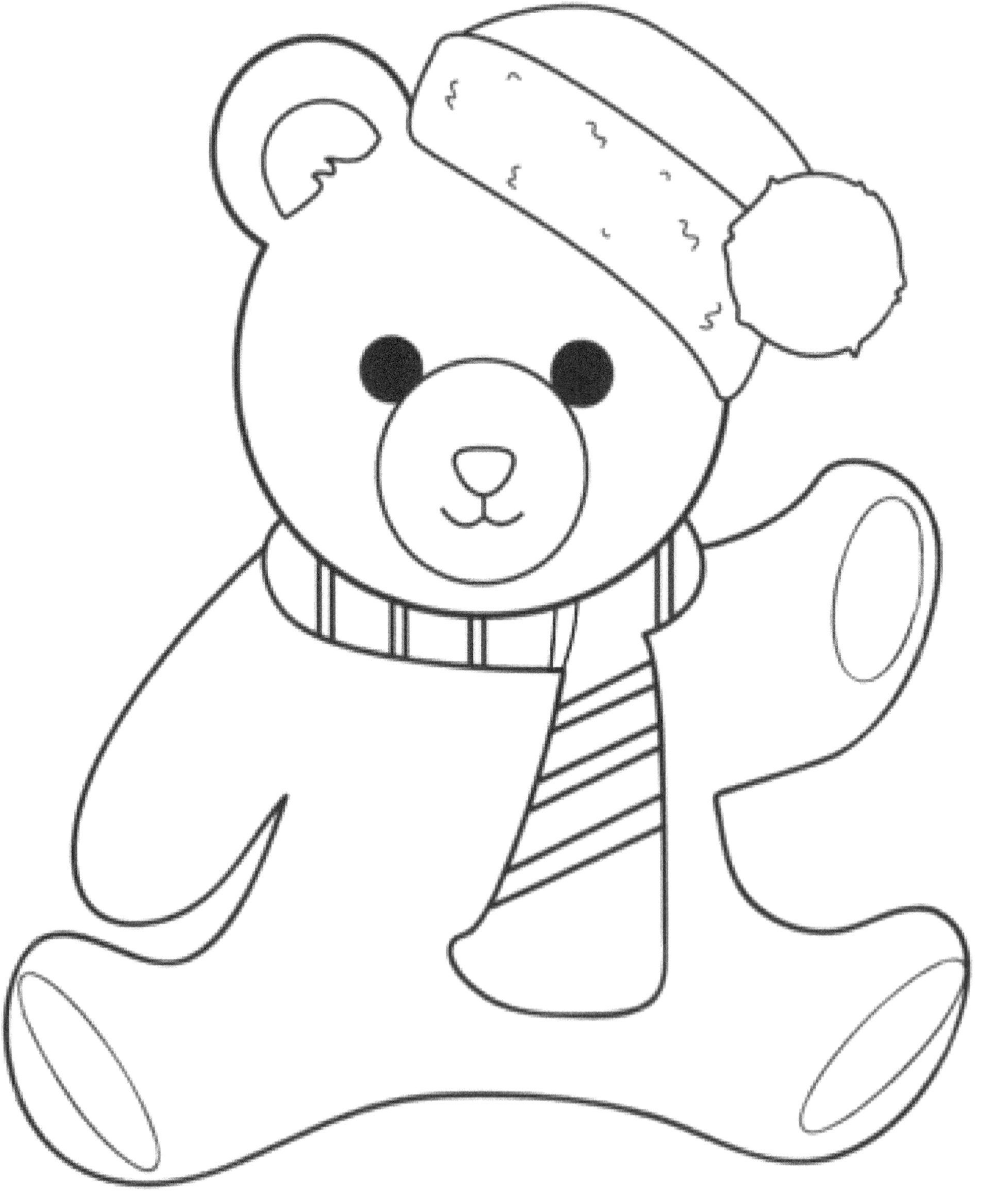

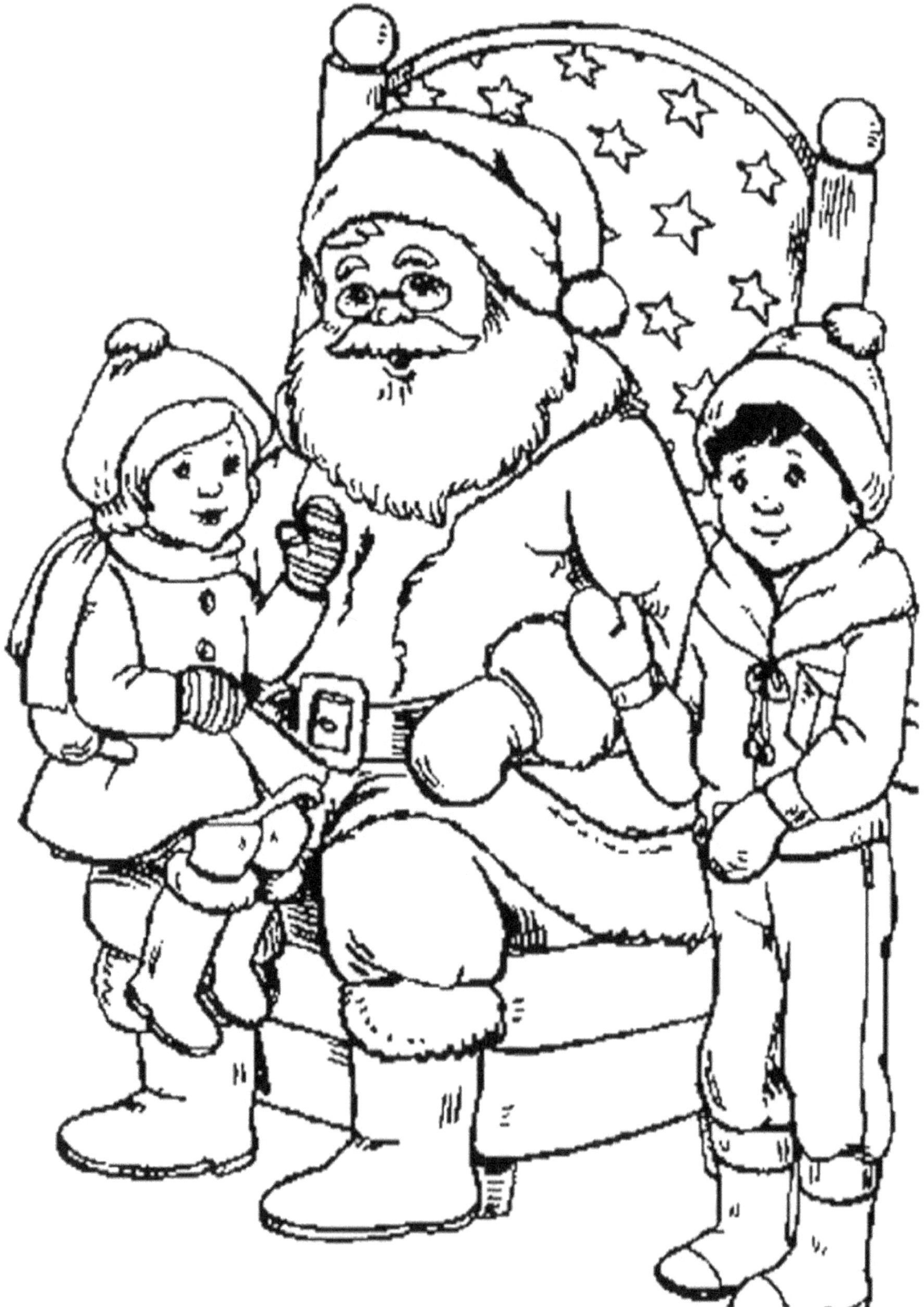

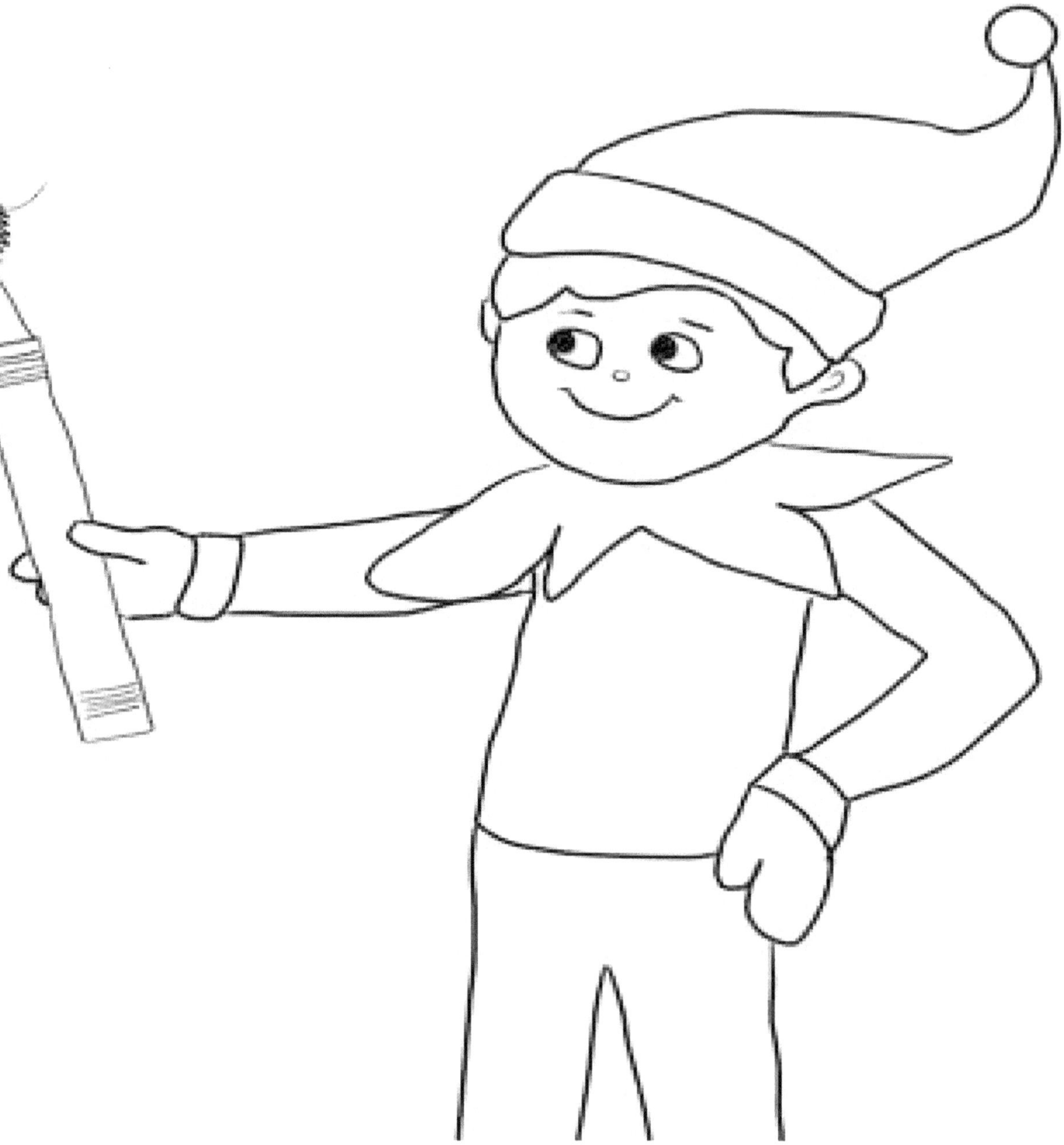

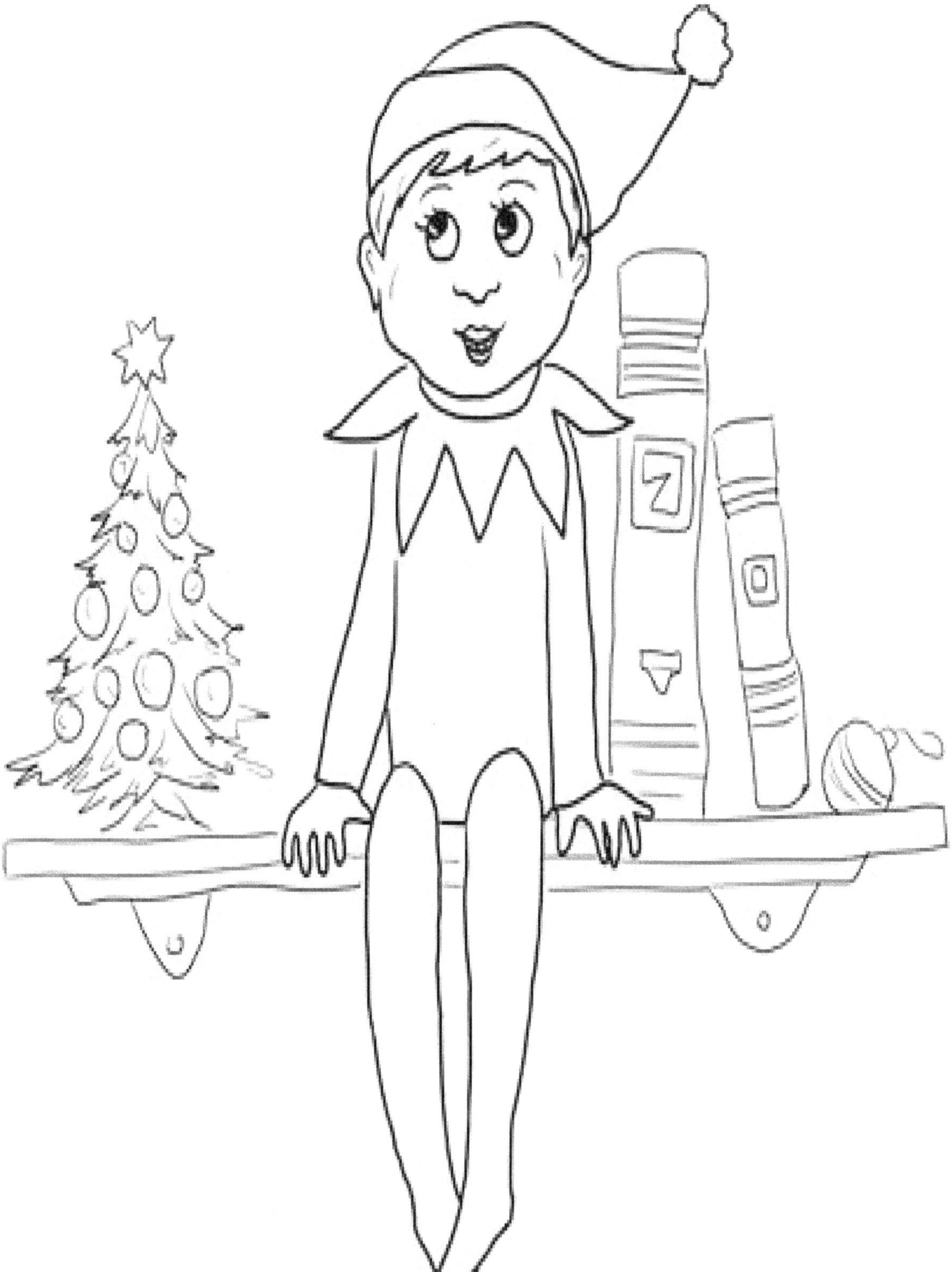

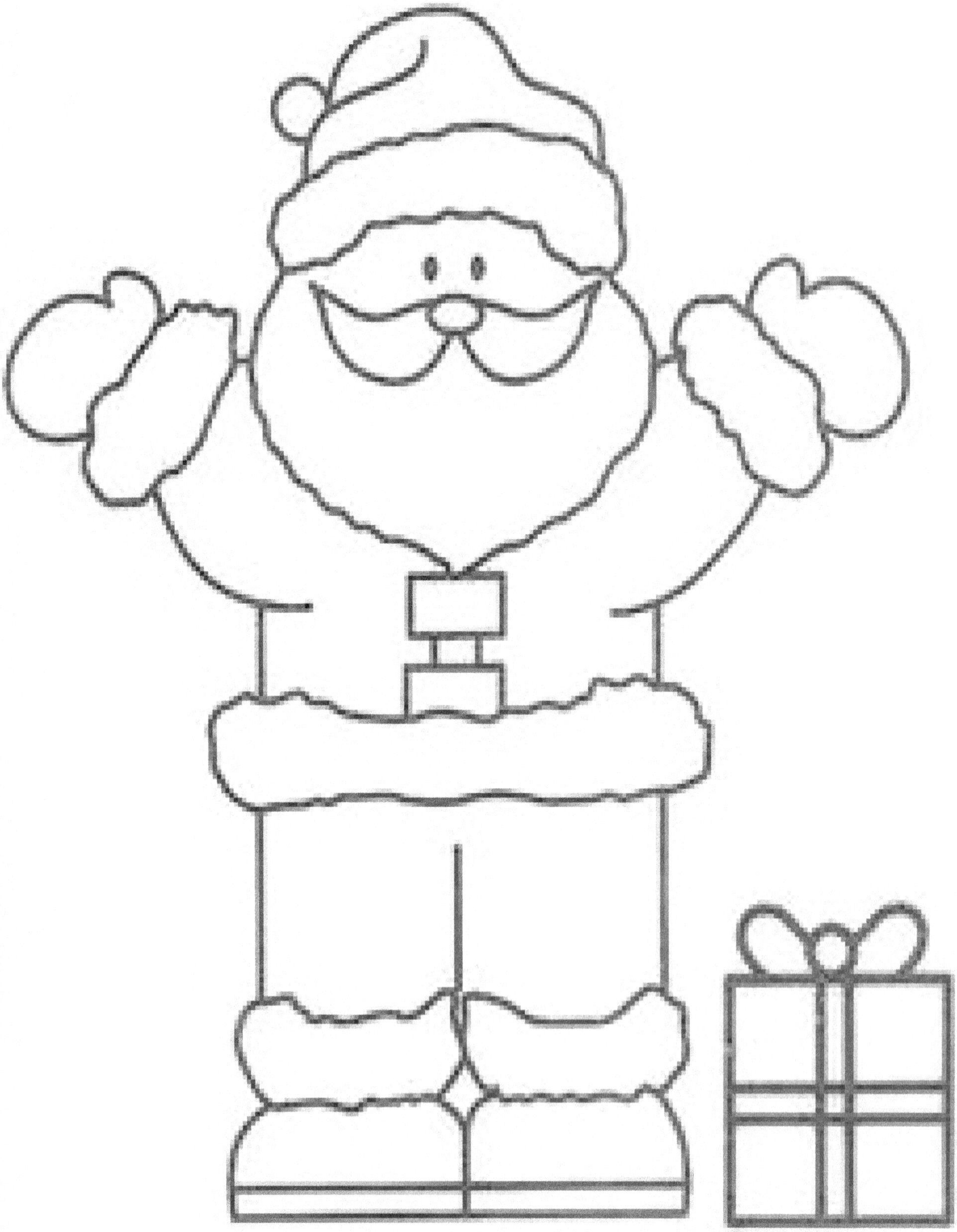

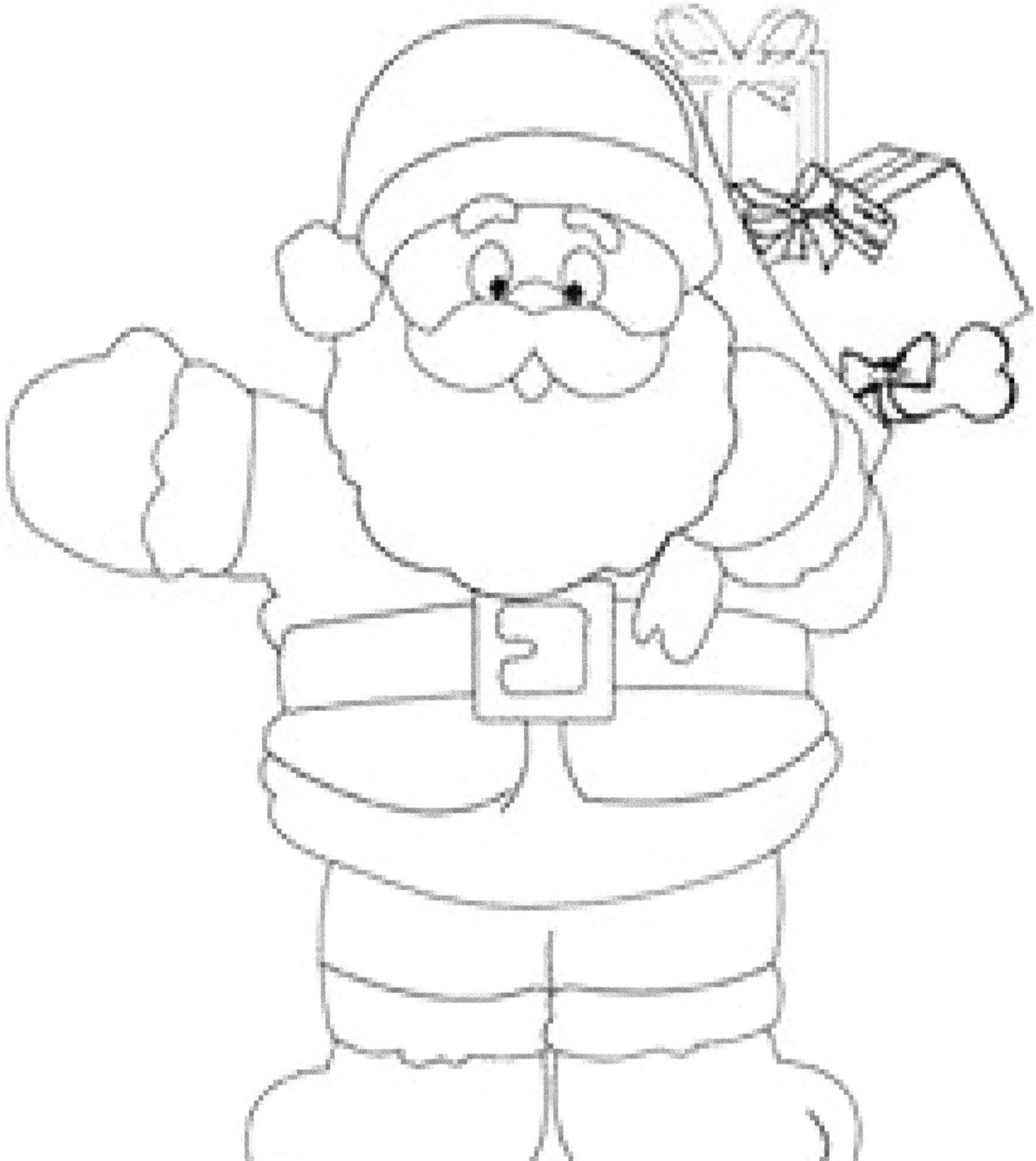

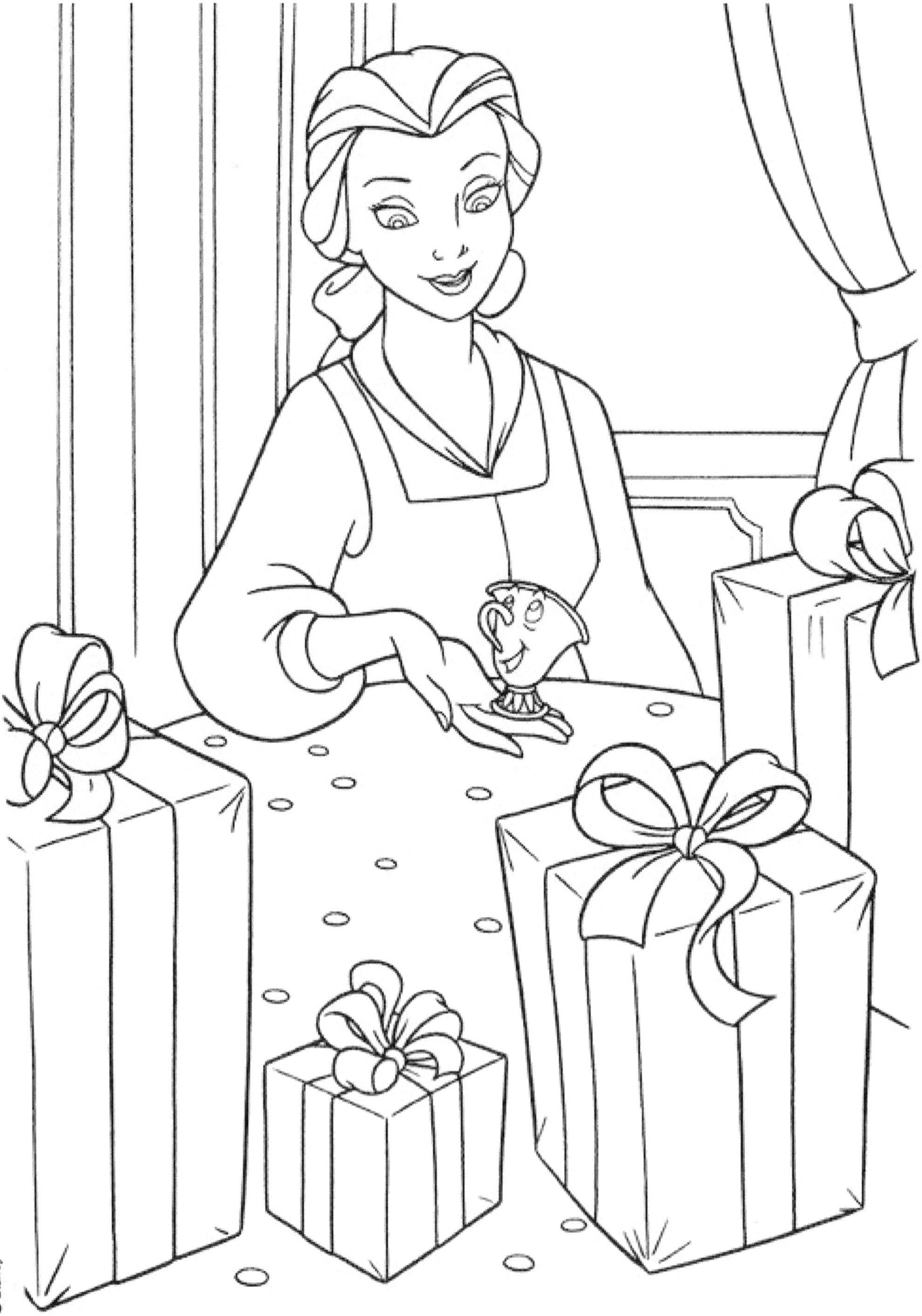

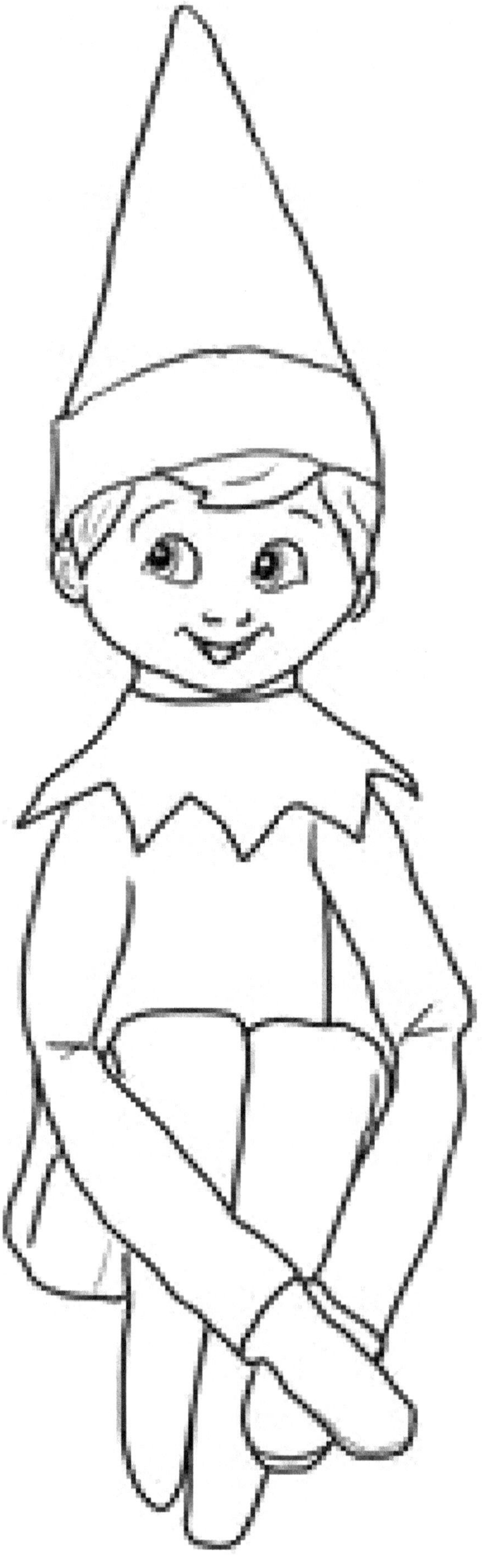

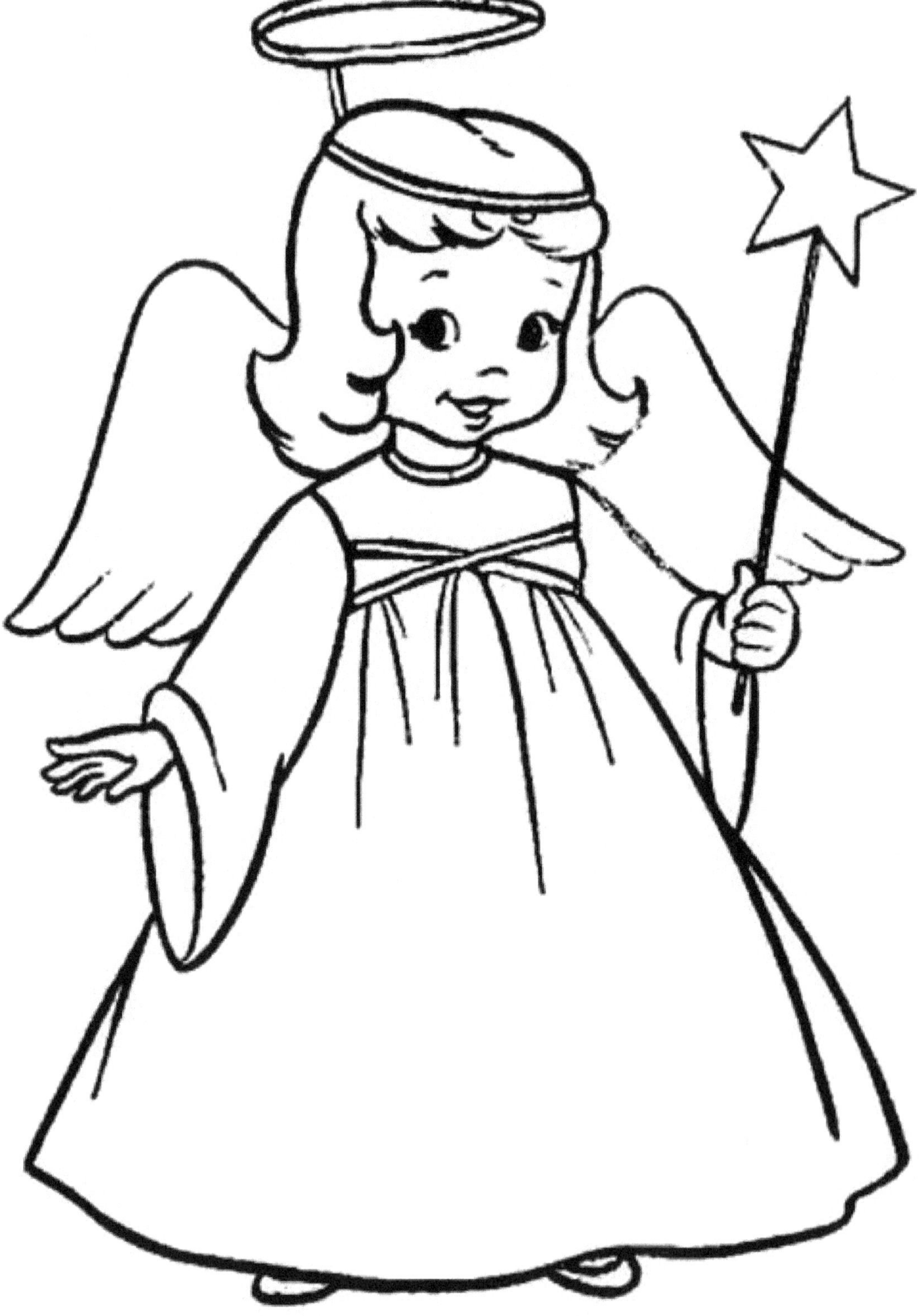

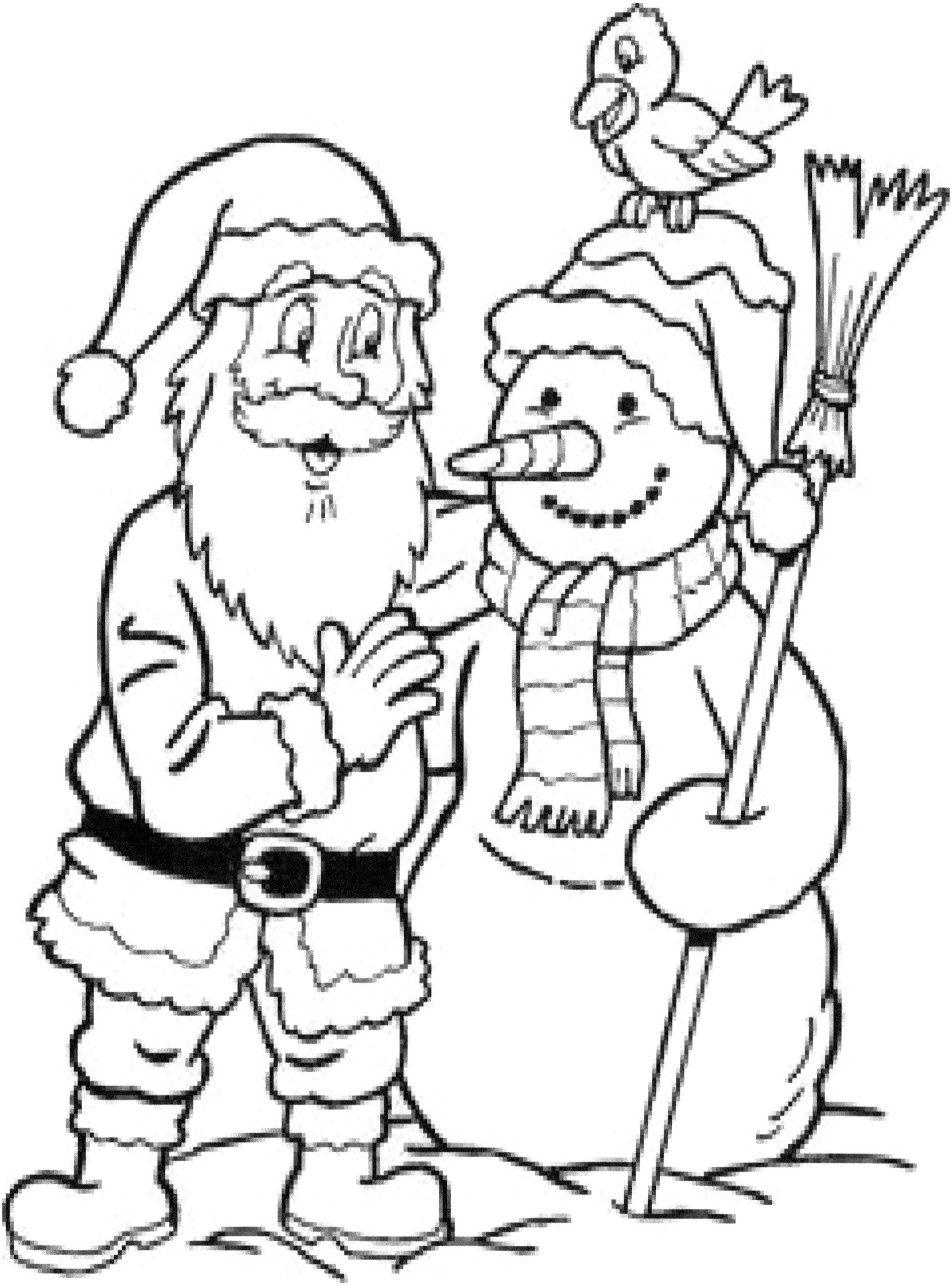

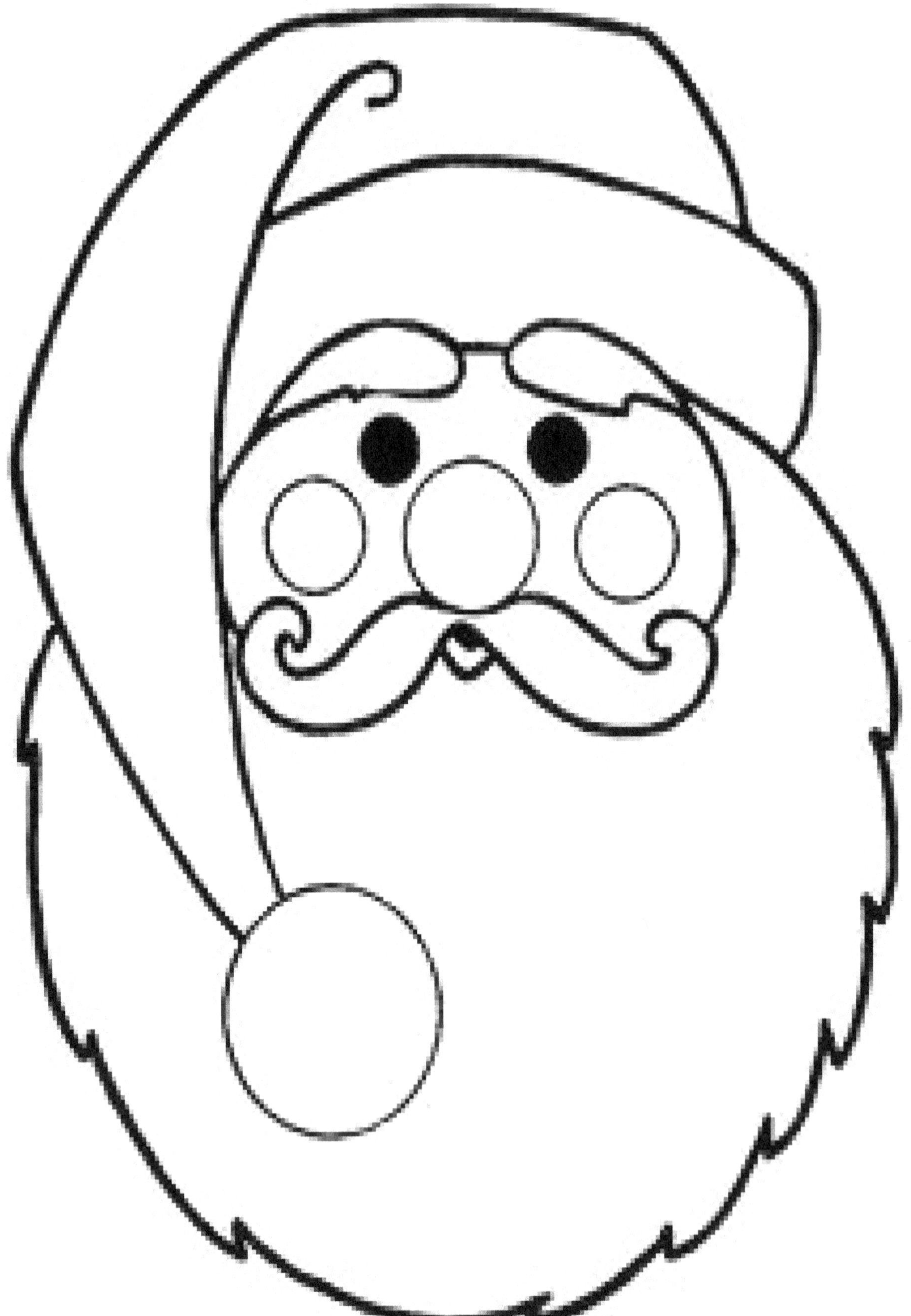

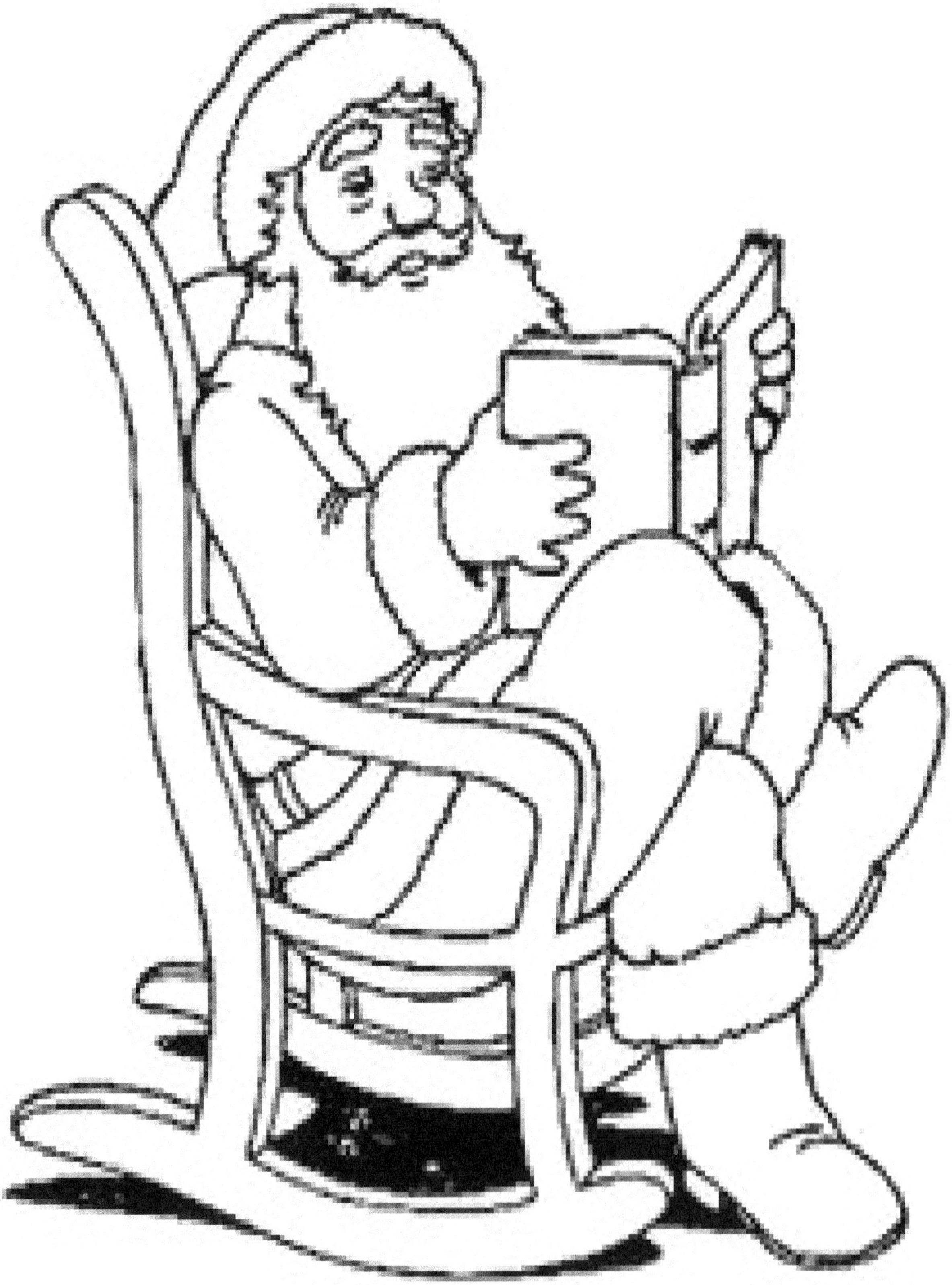

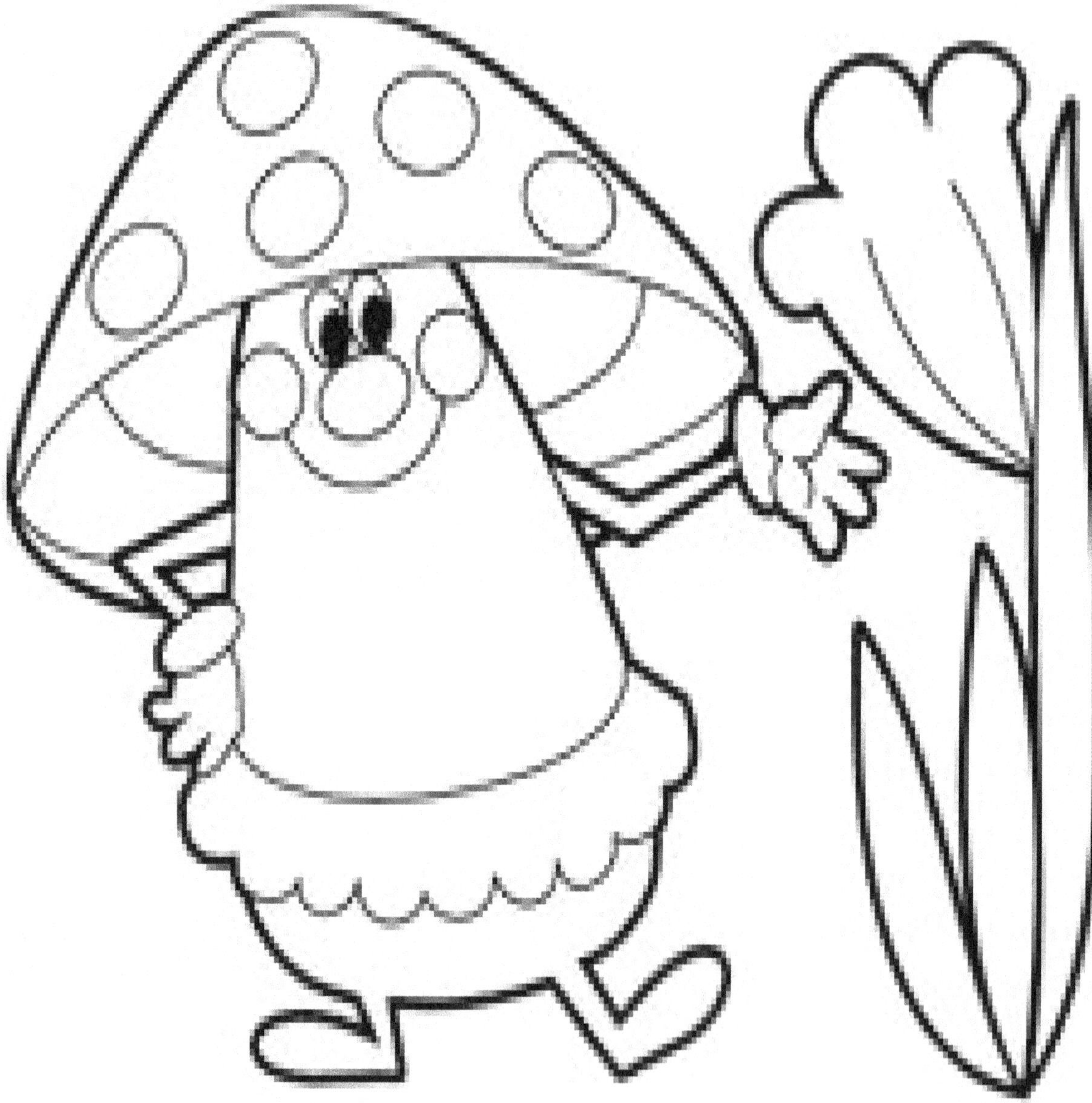

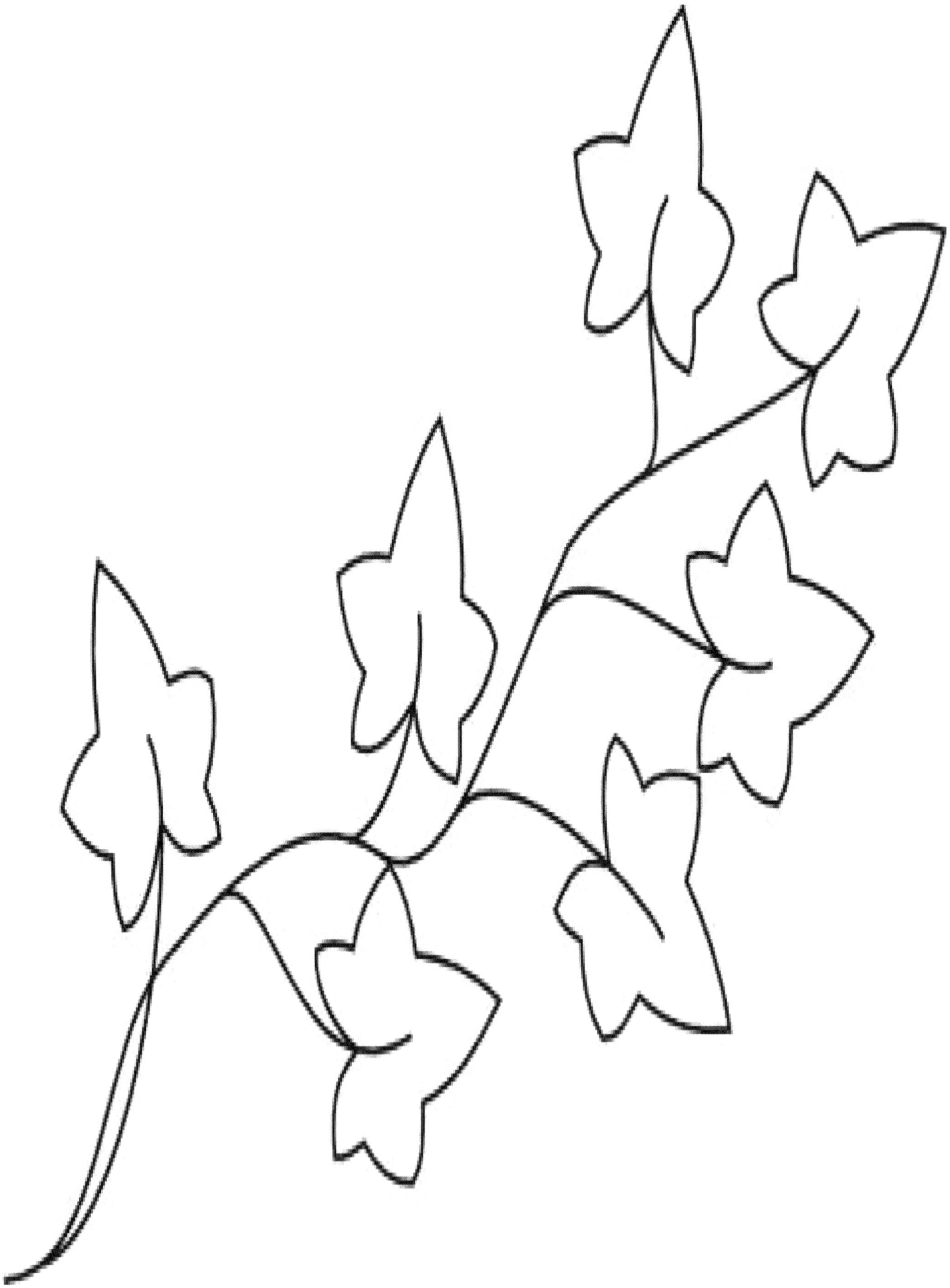

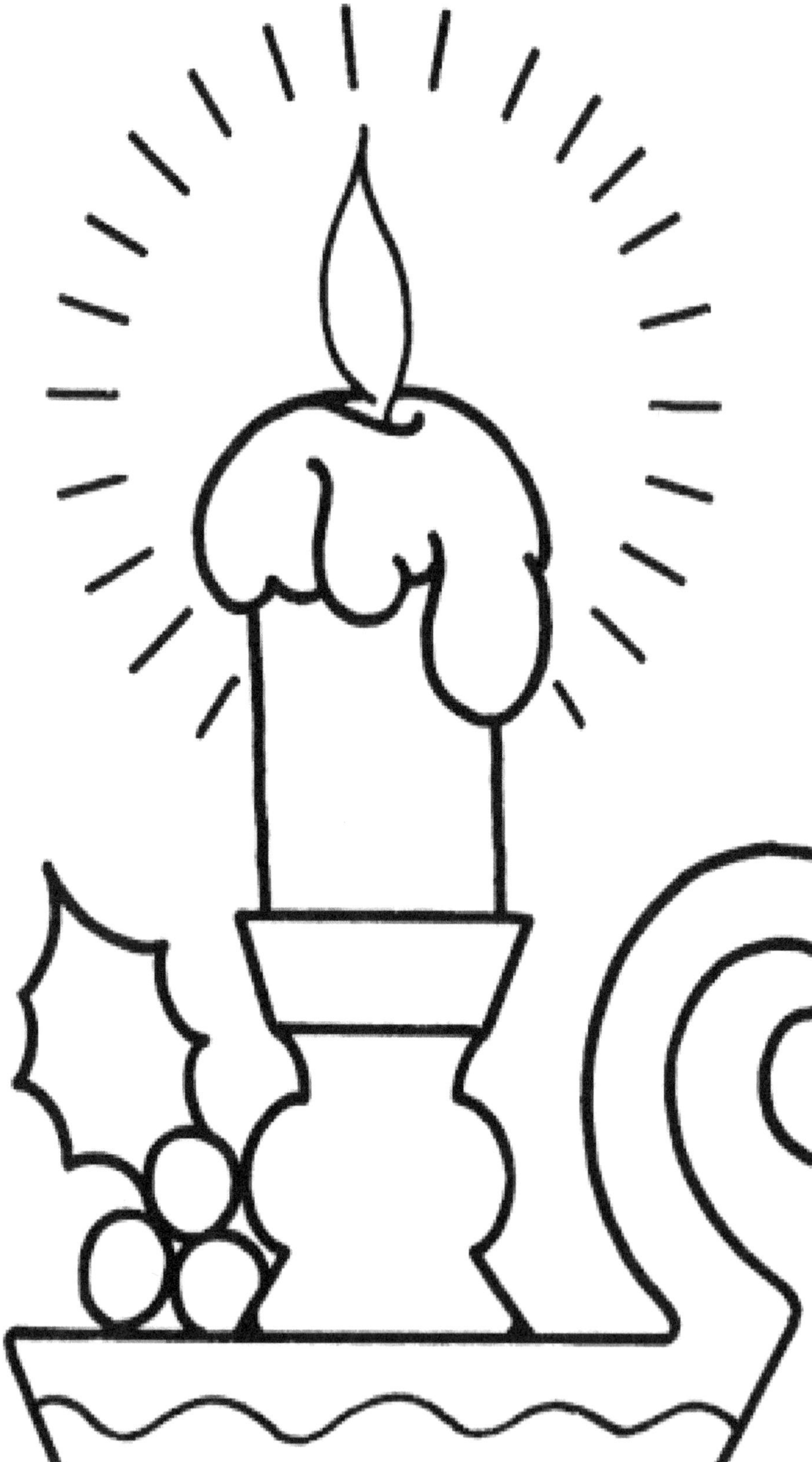

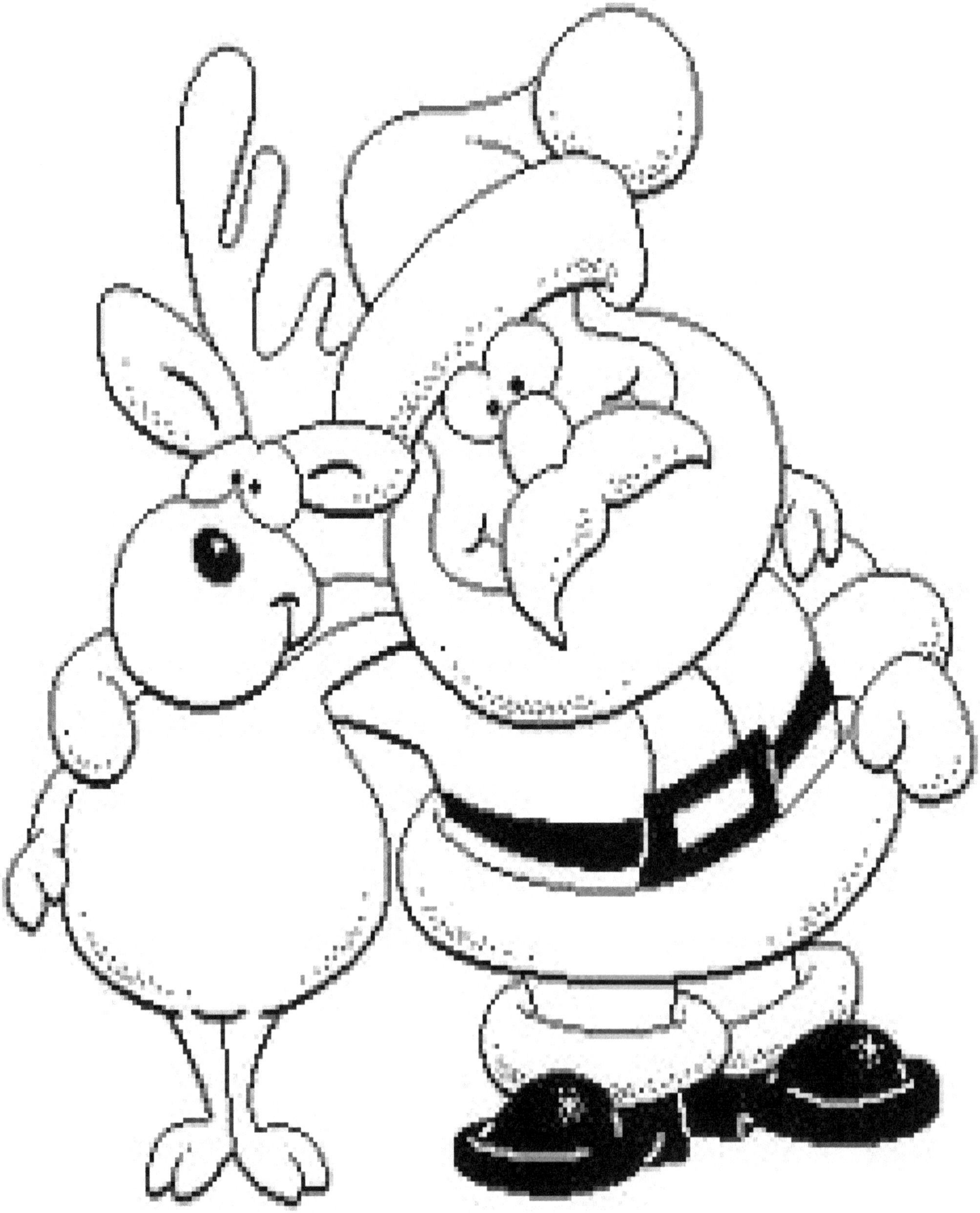

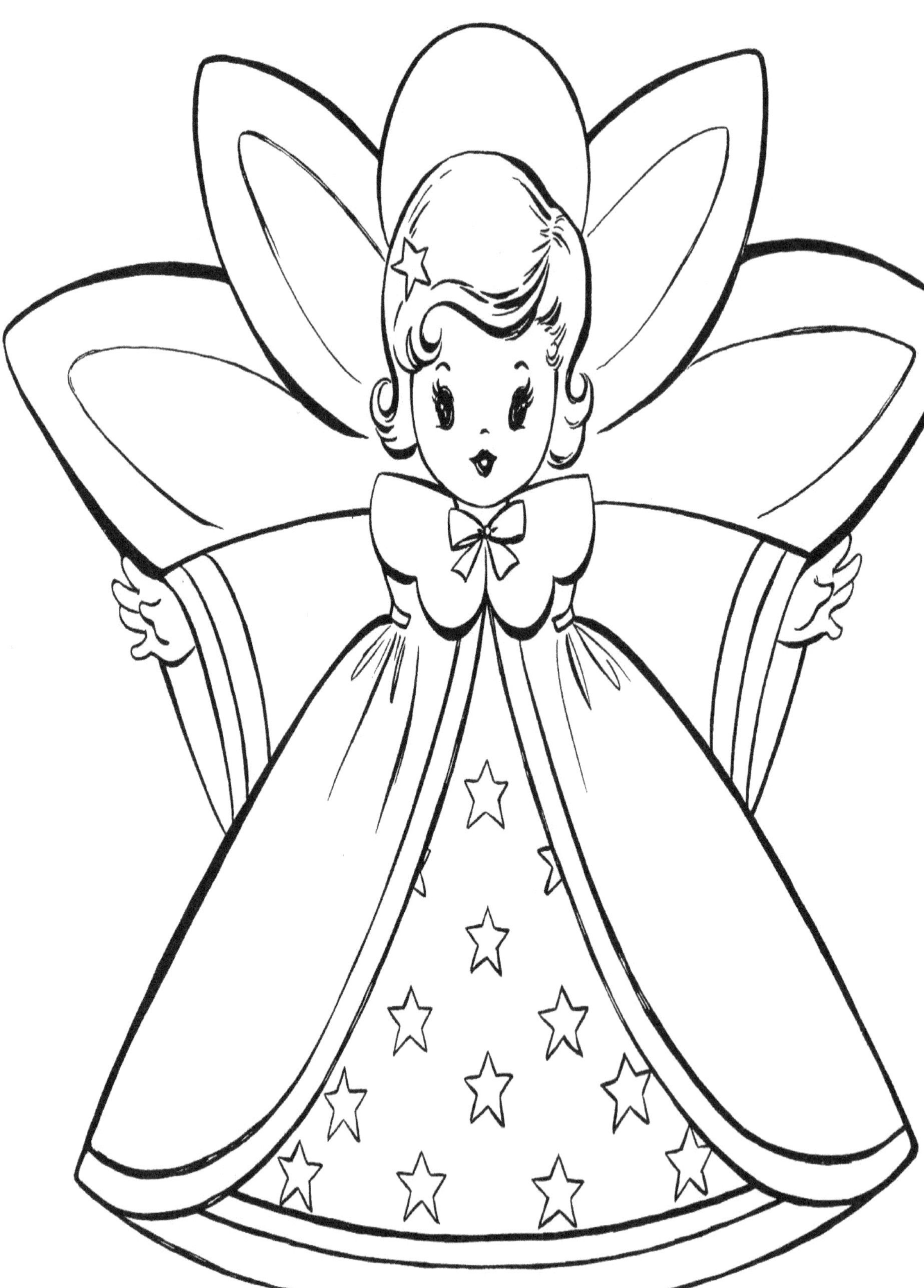

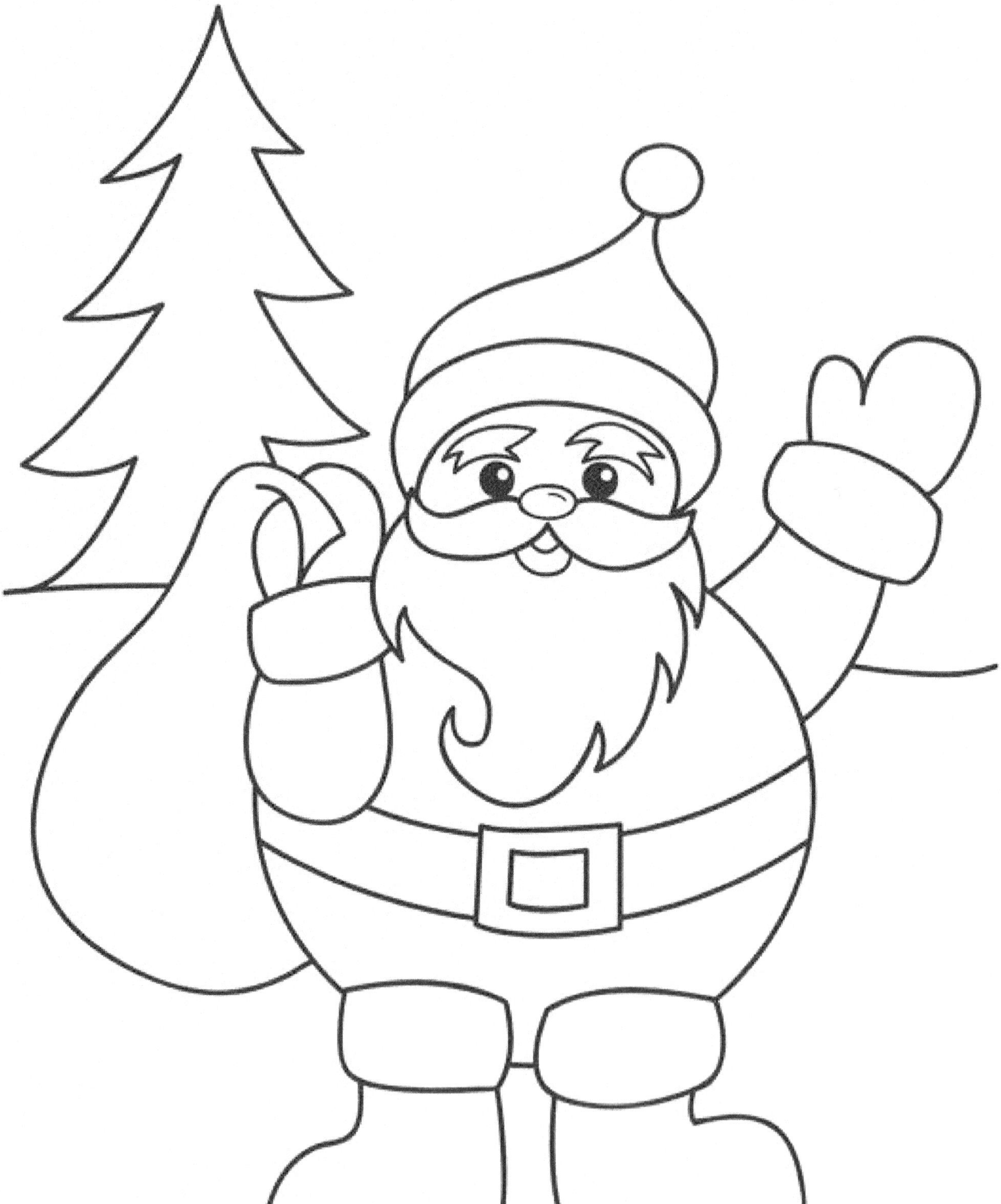

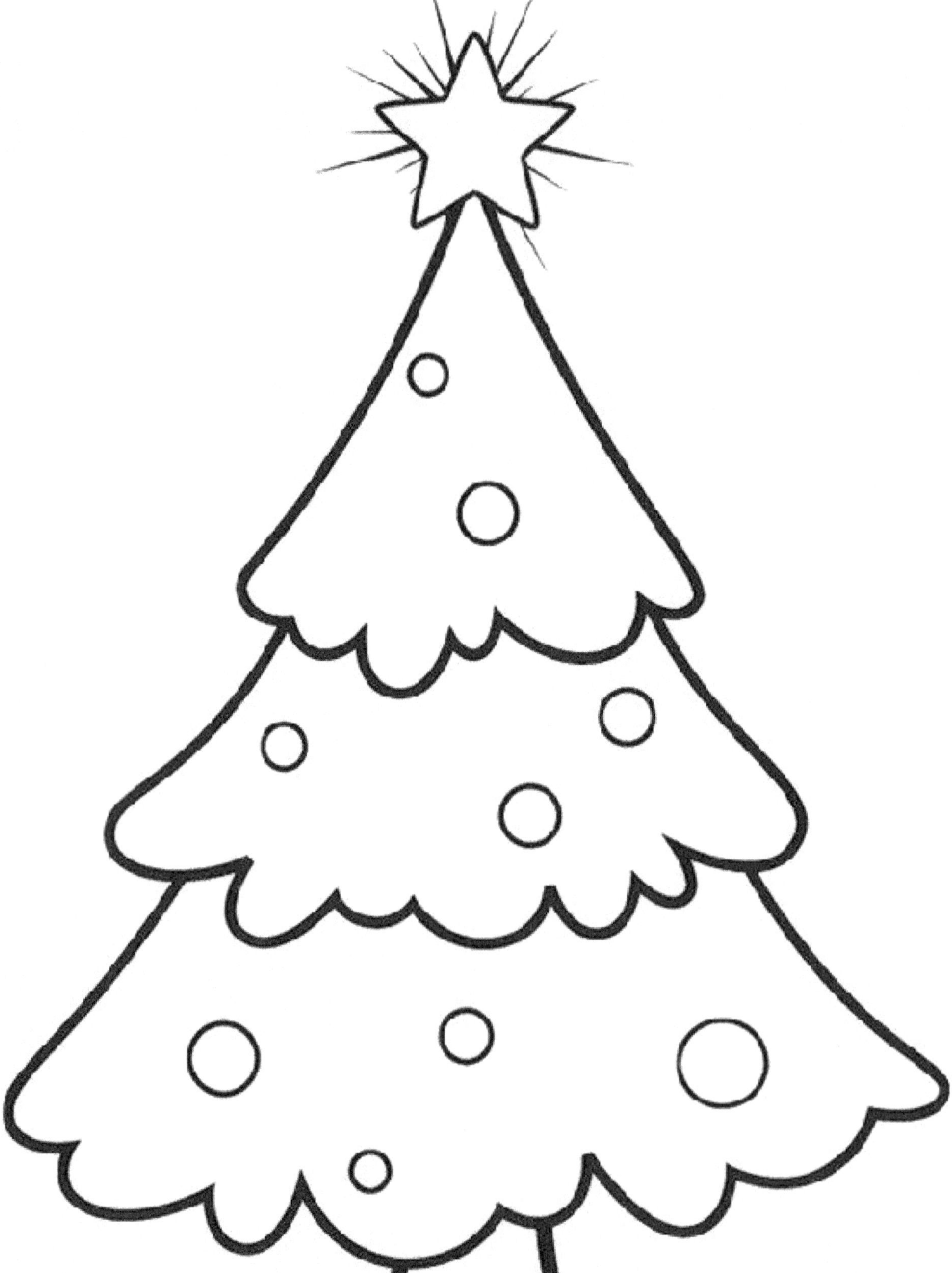

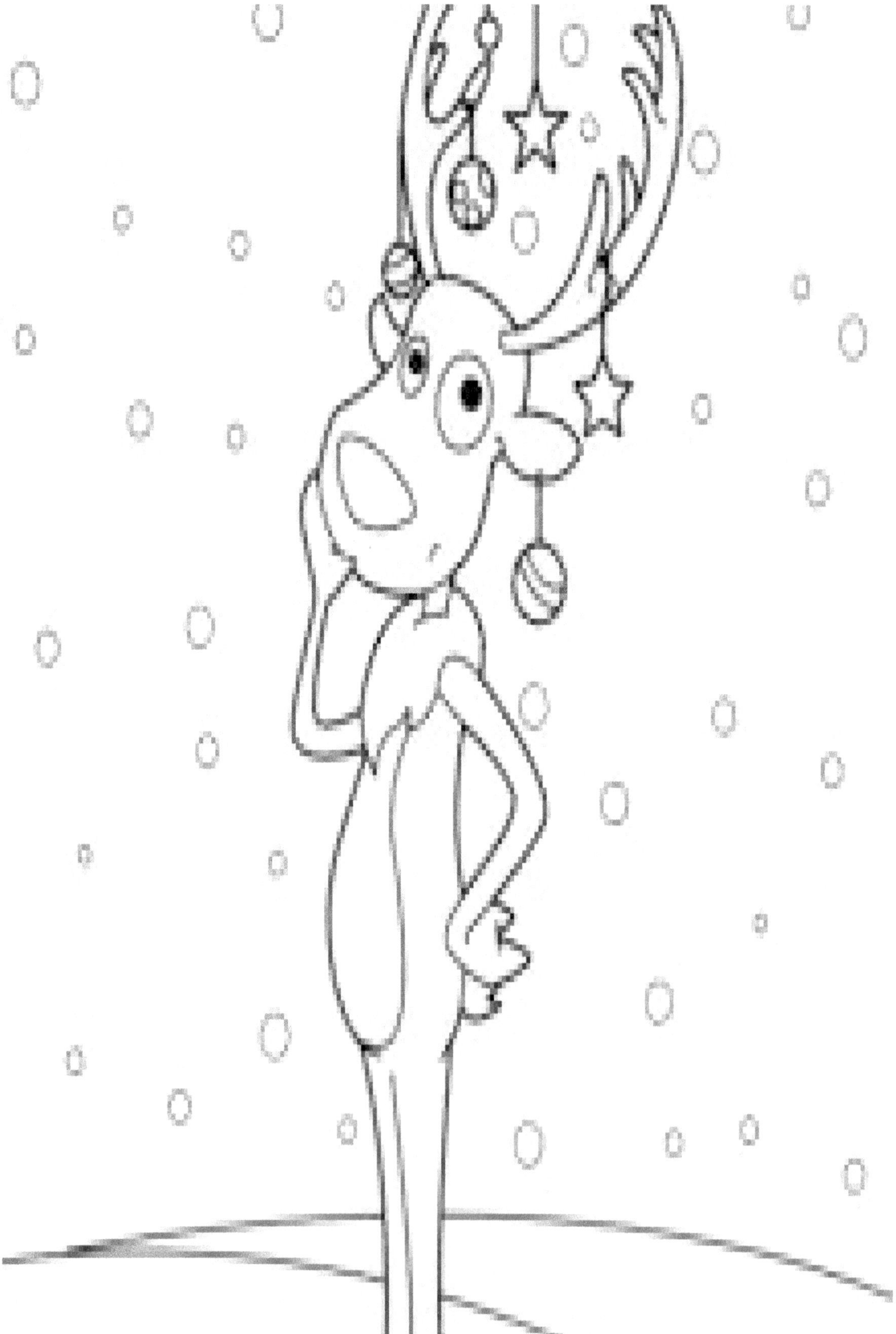

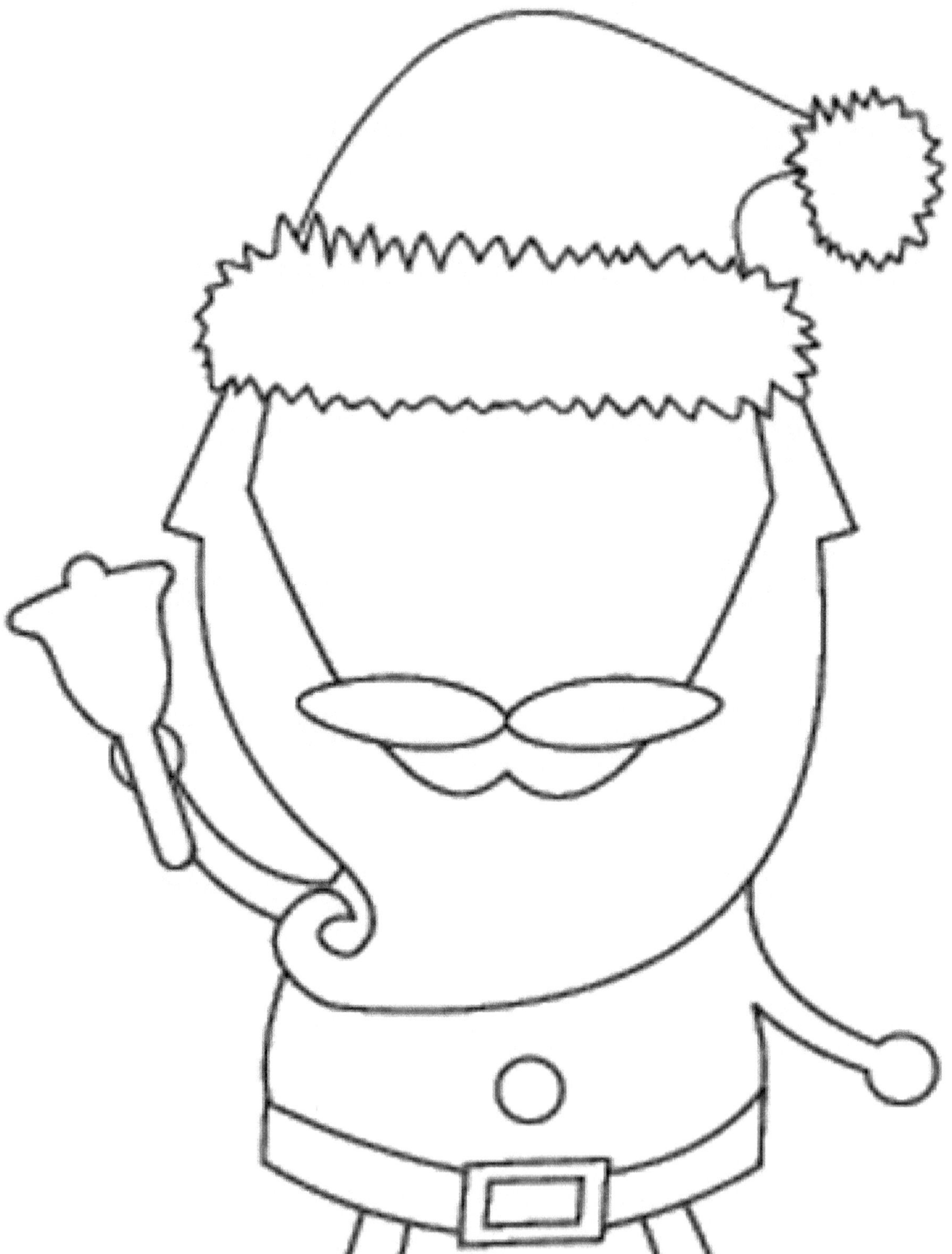

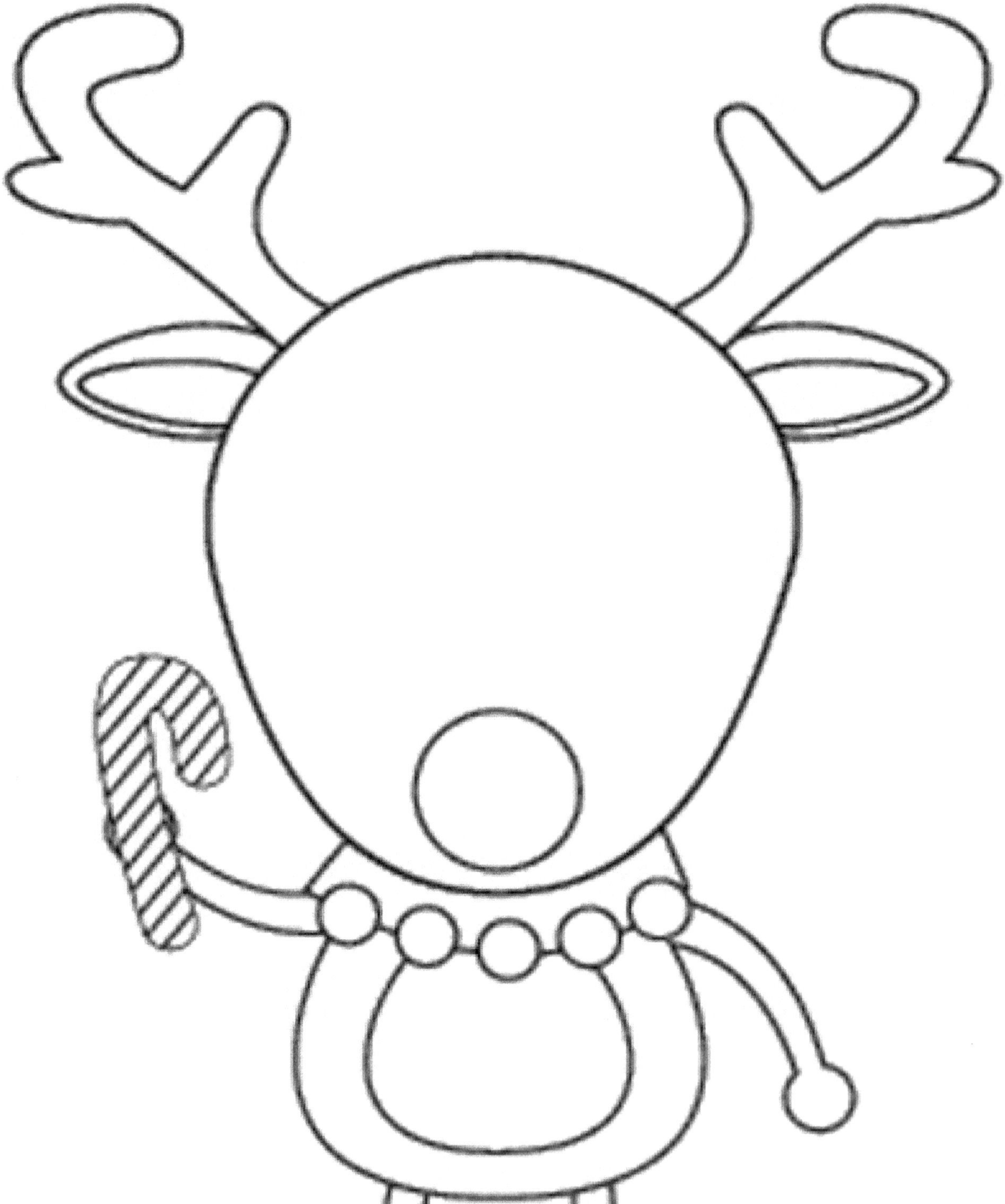

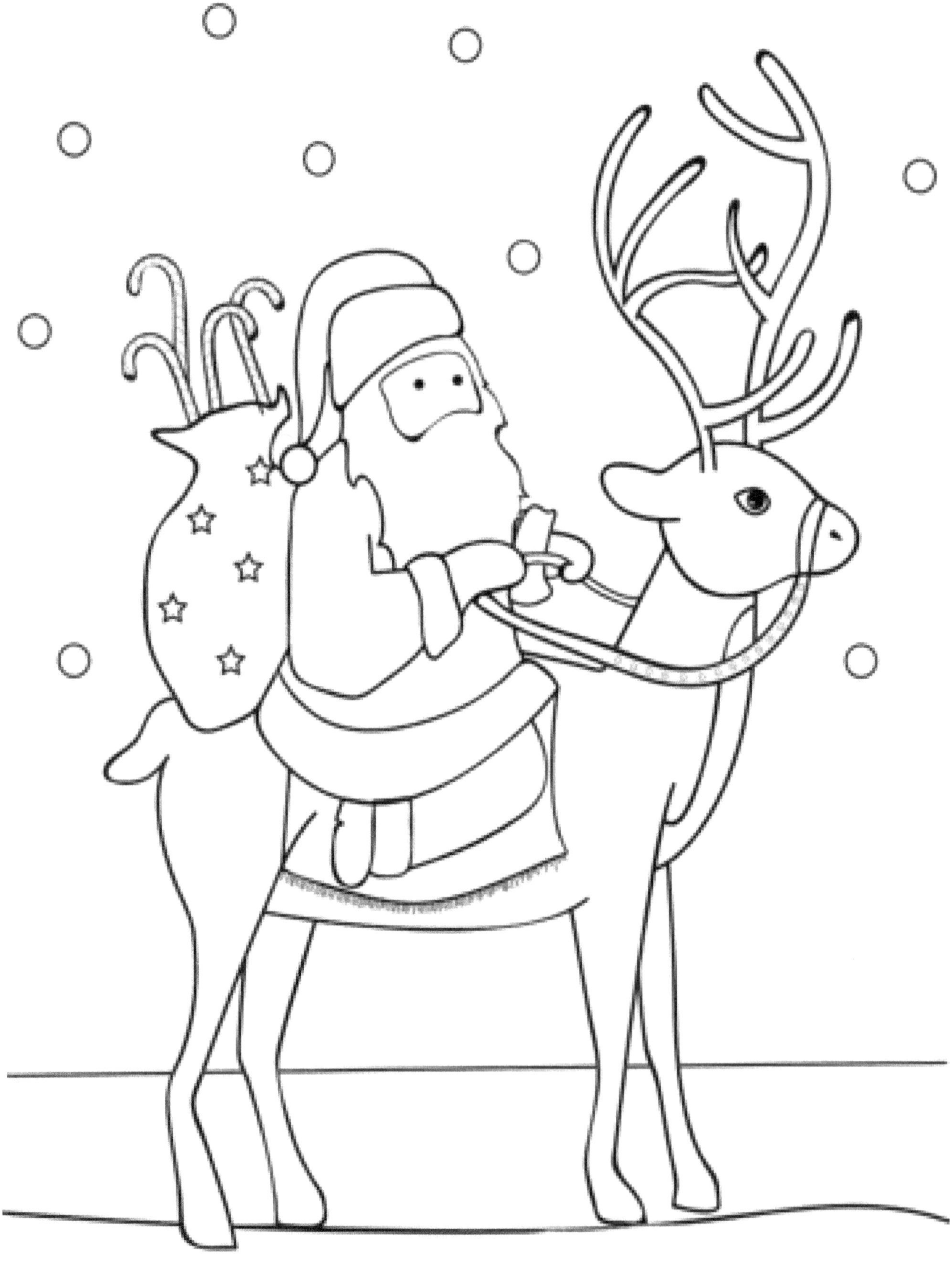

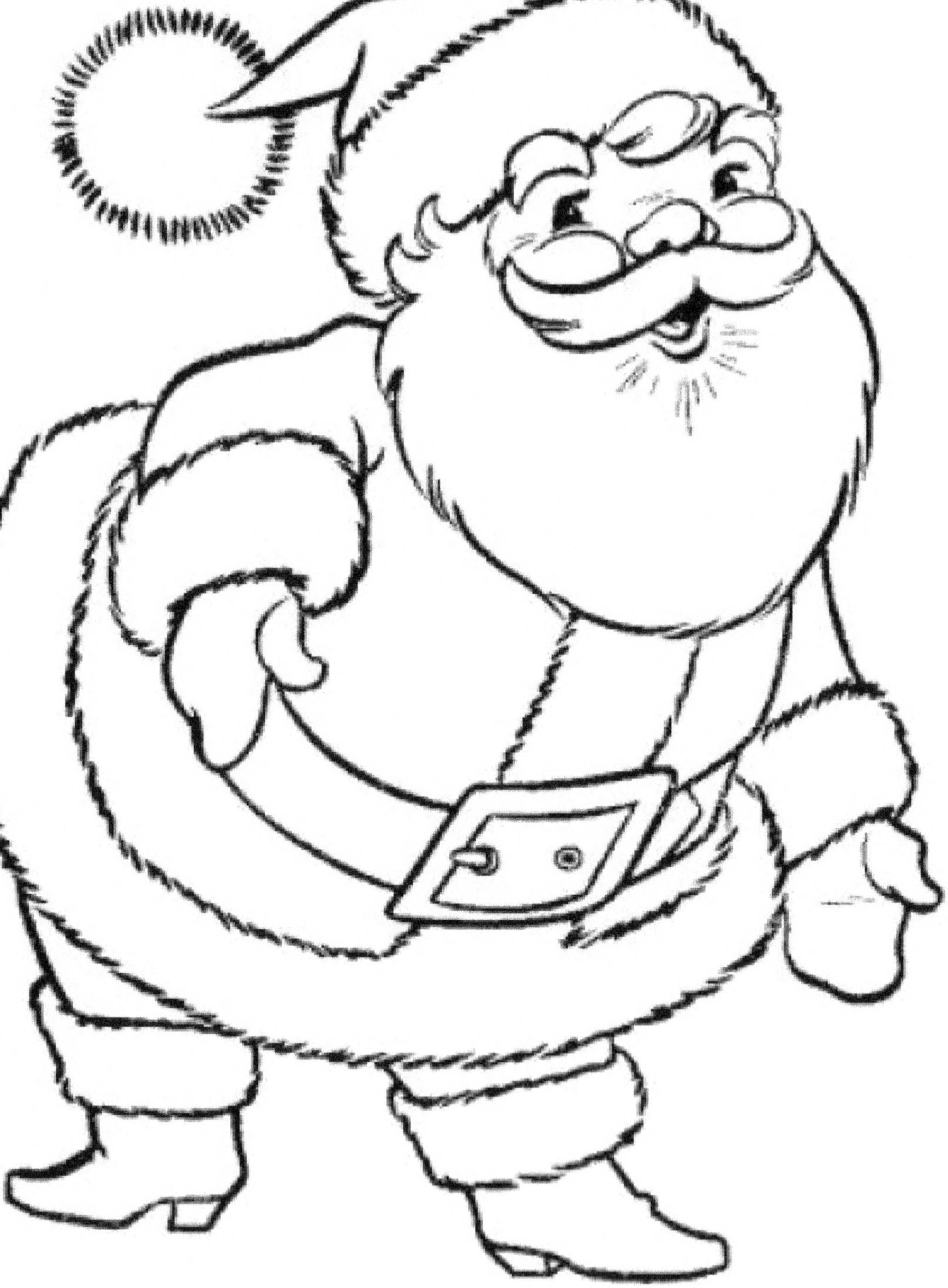

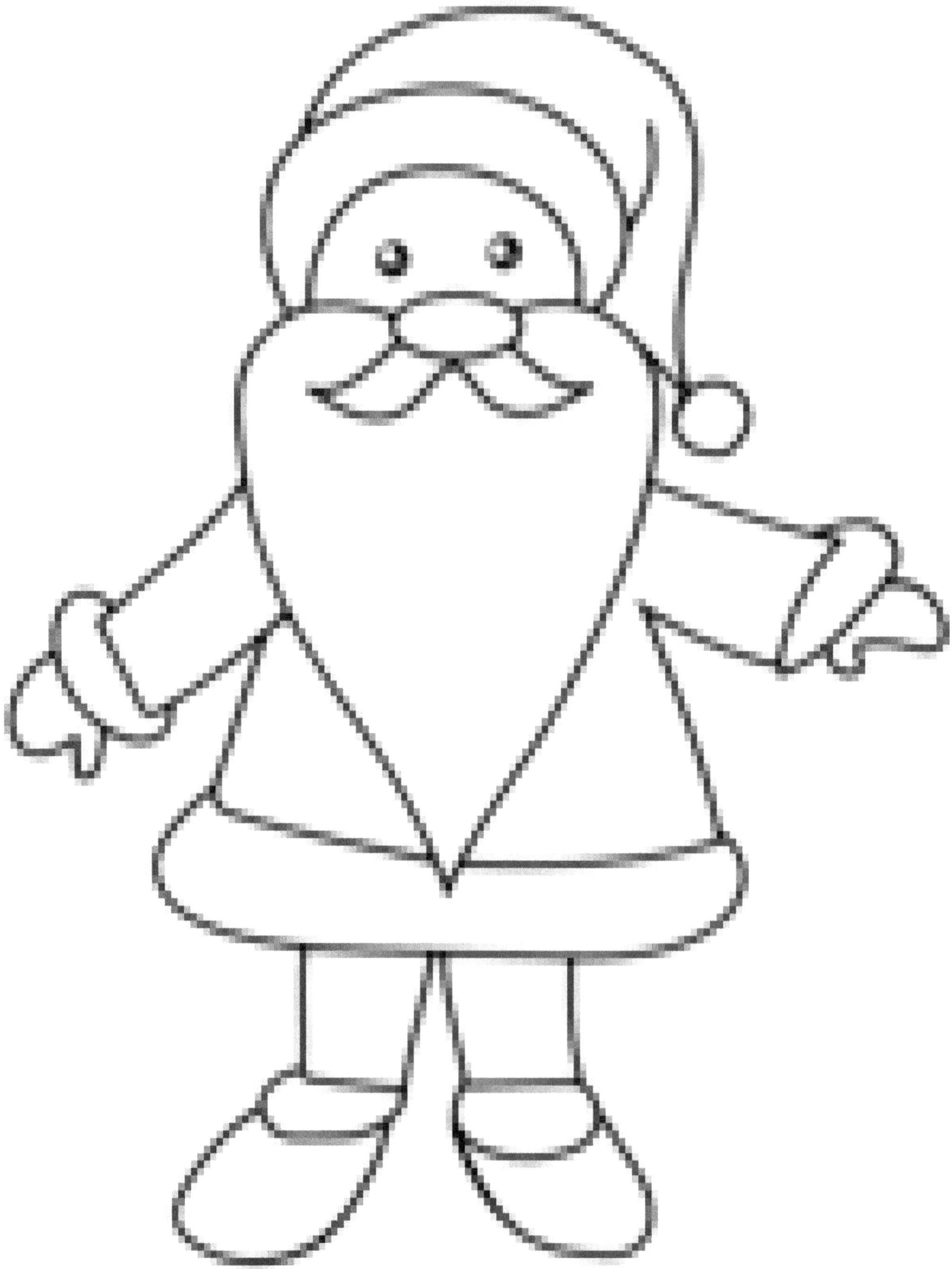

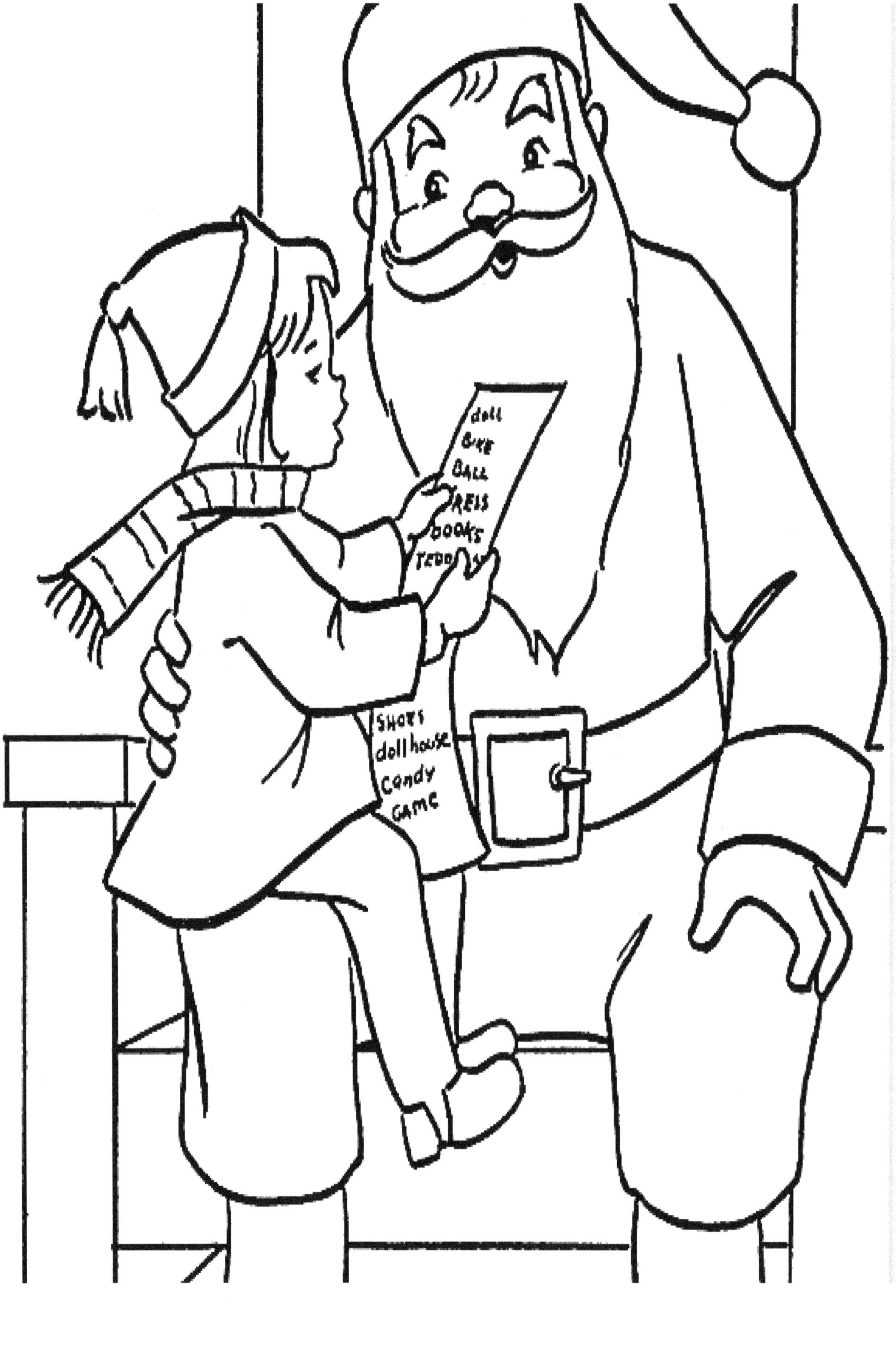
doll
BALL
BOOKS
SHOES
dollhouse
Candy
GAME

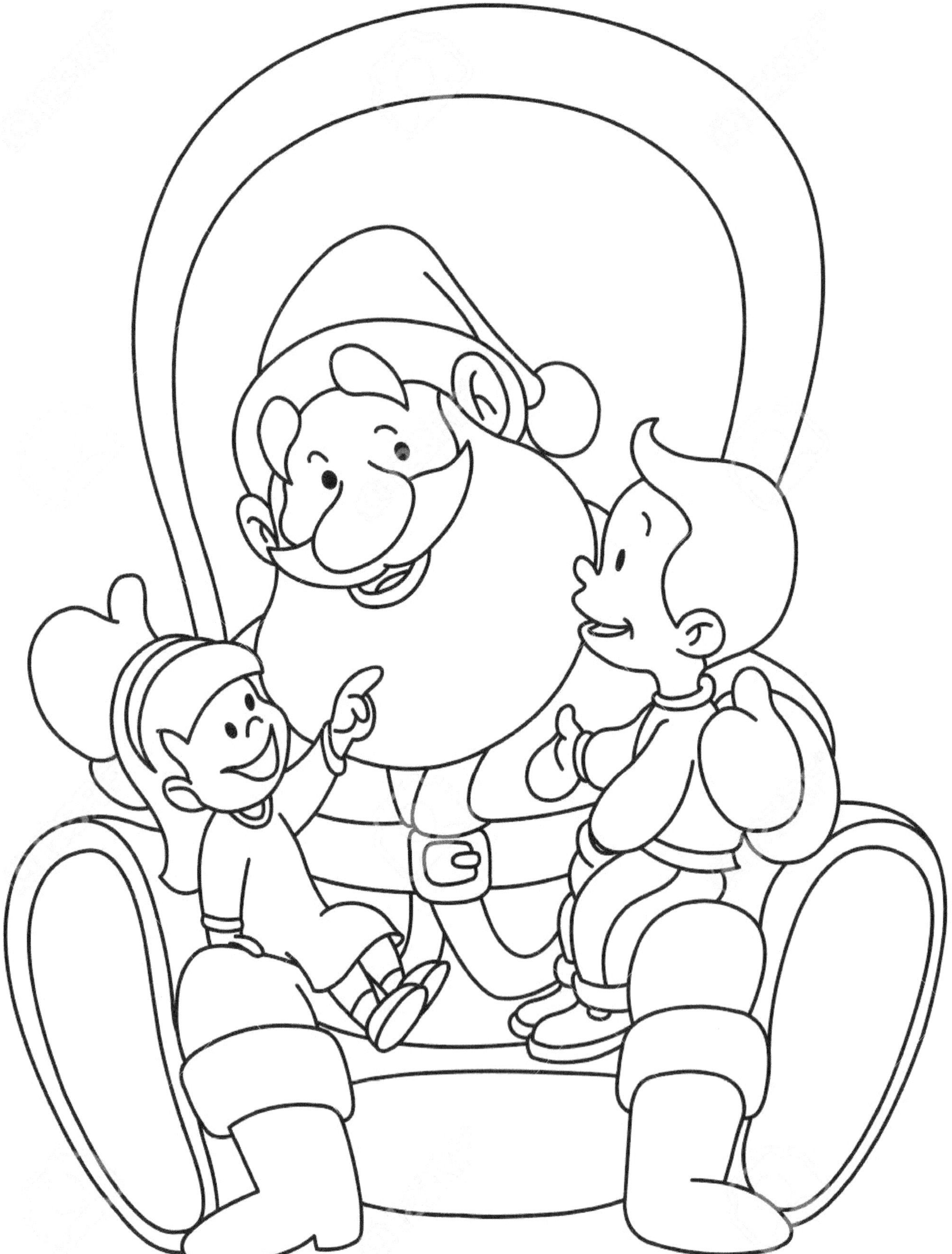

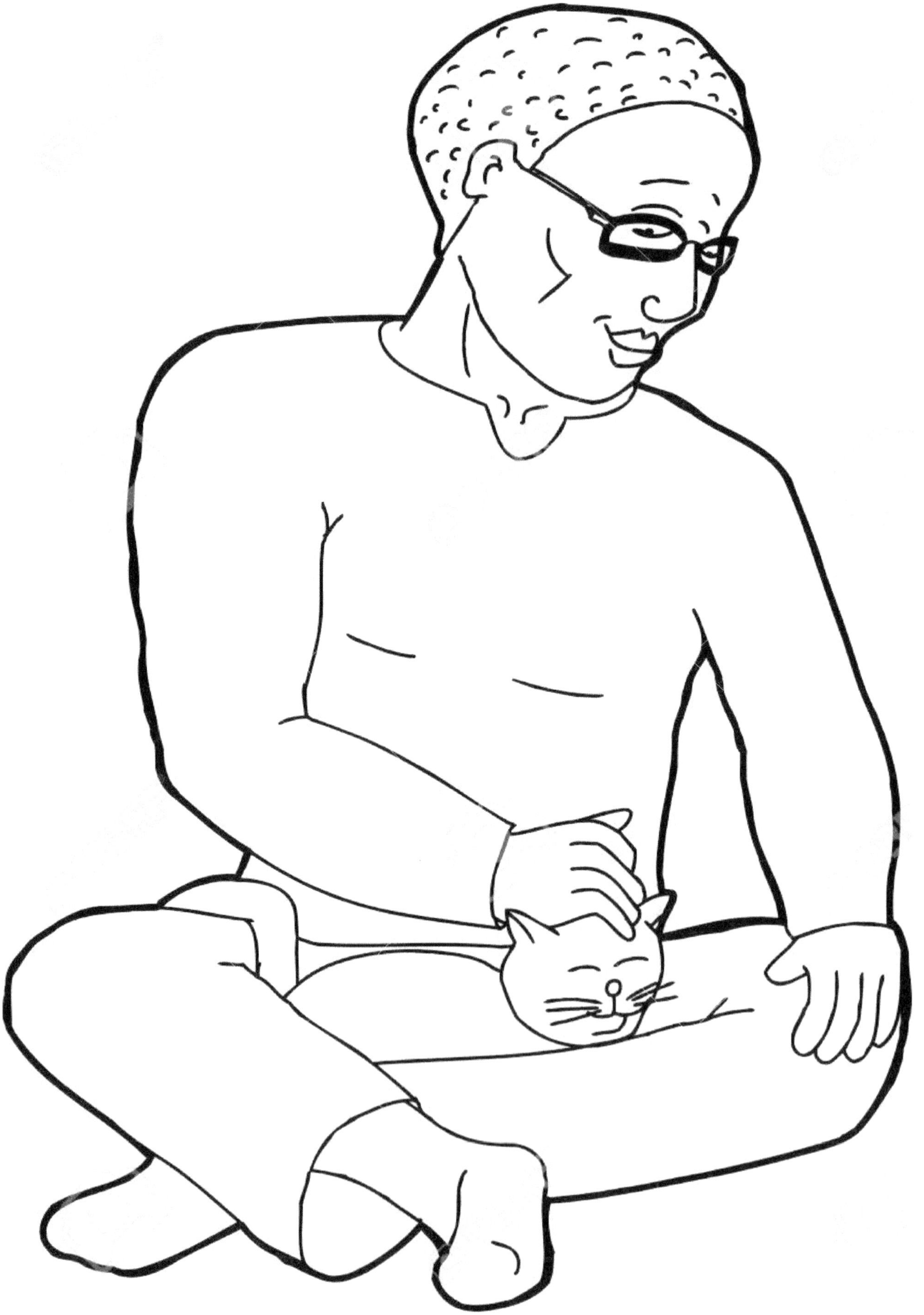

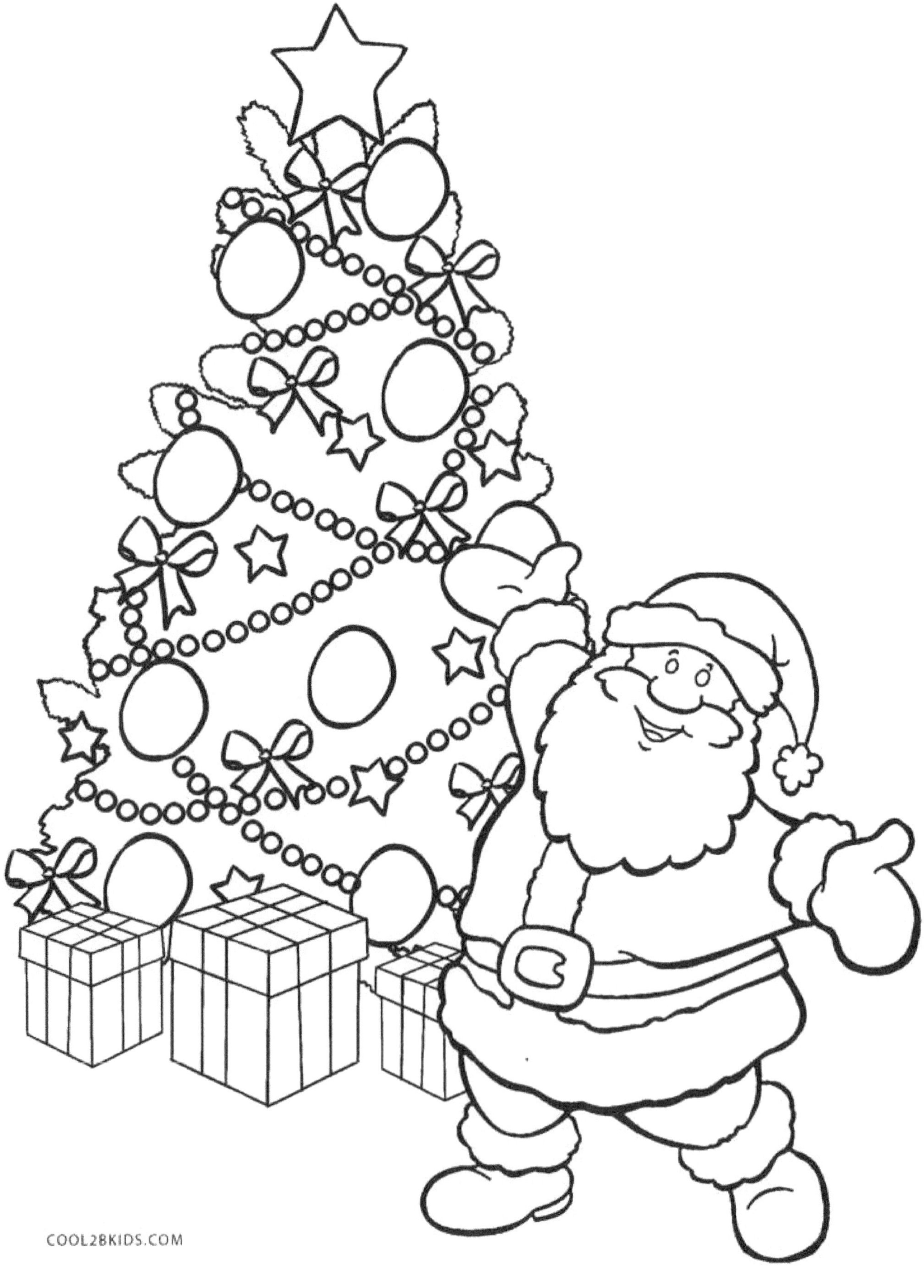

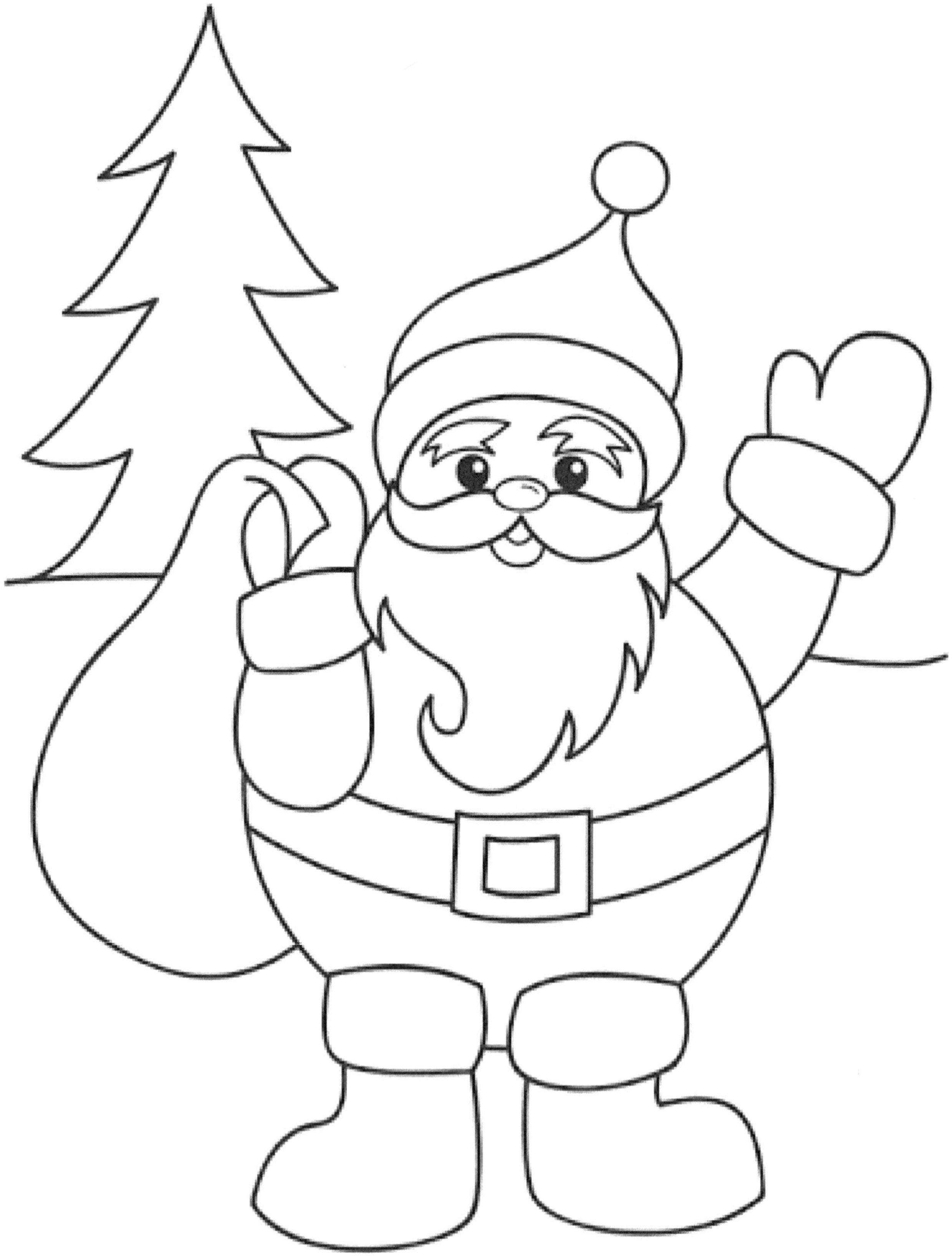

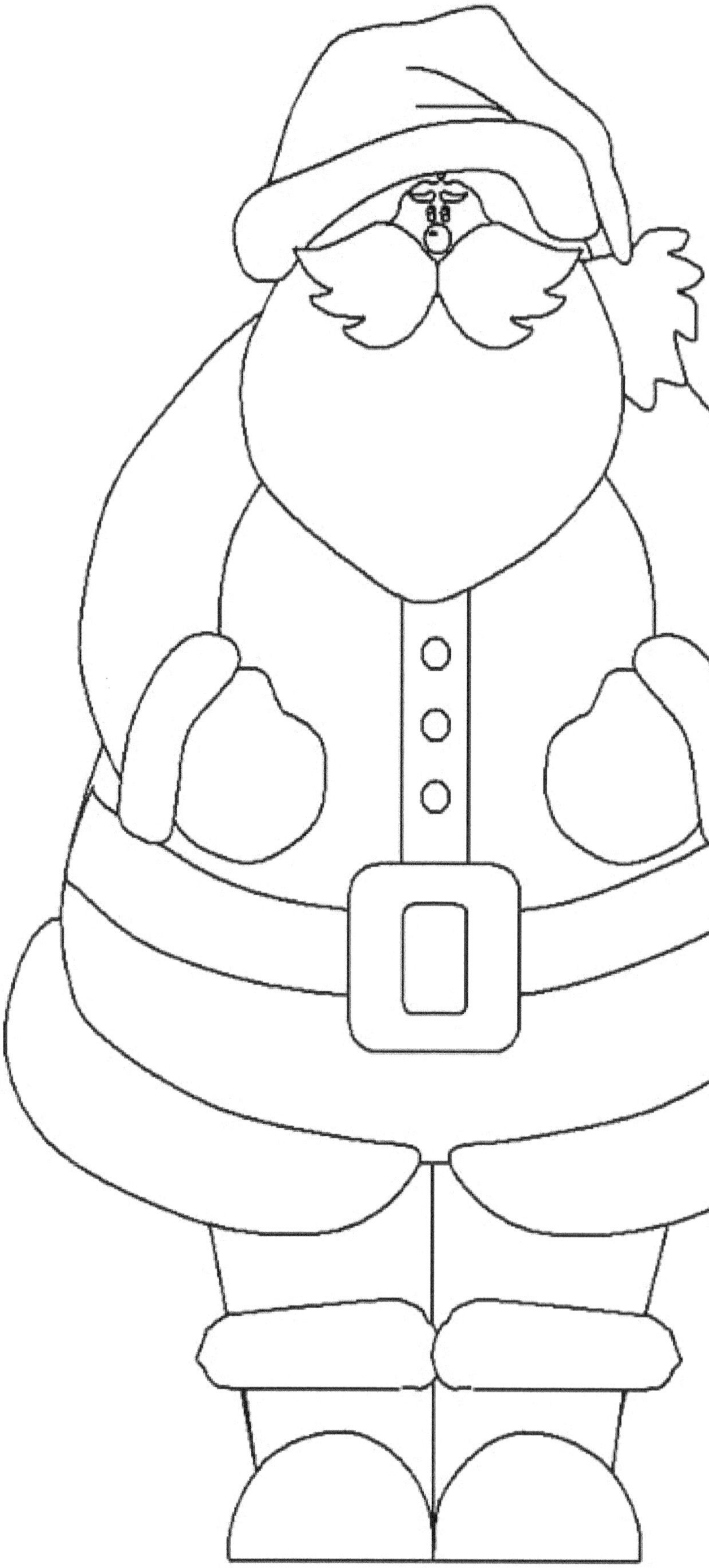

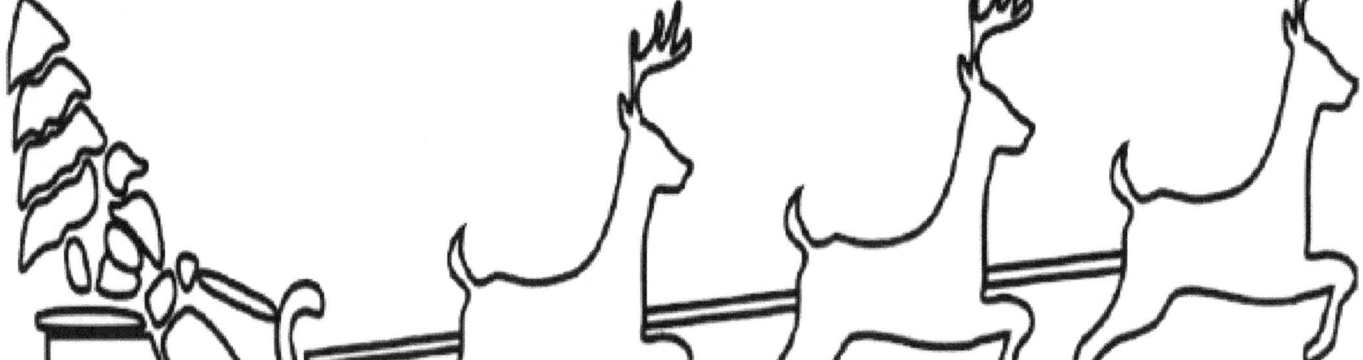

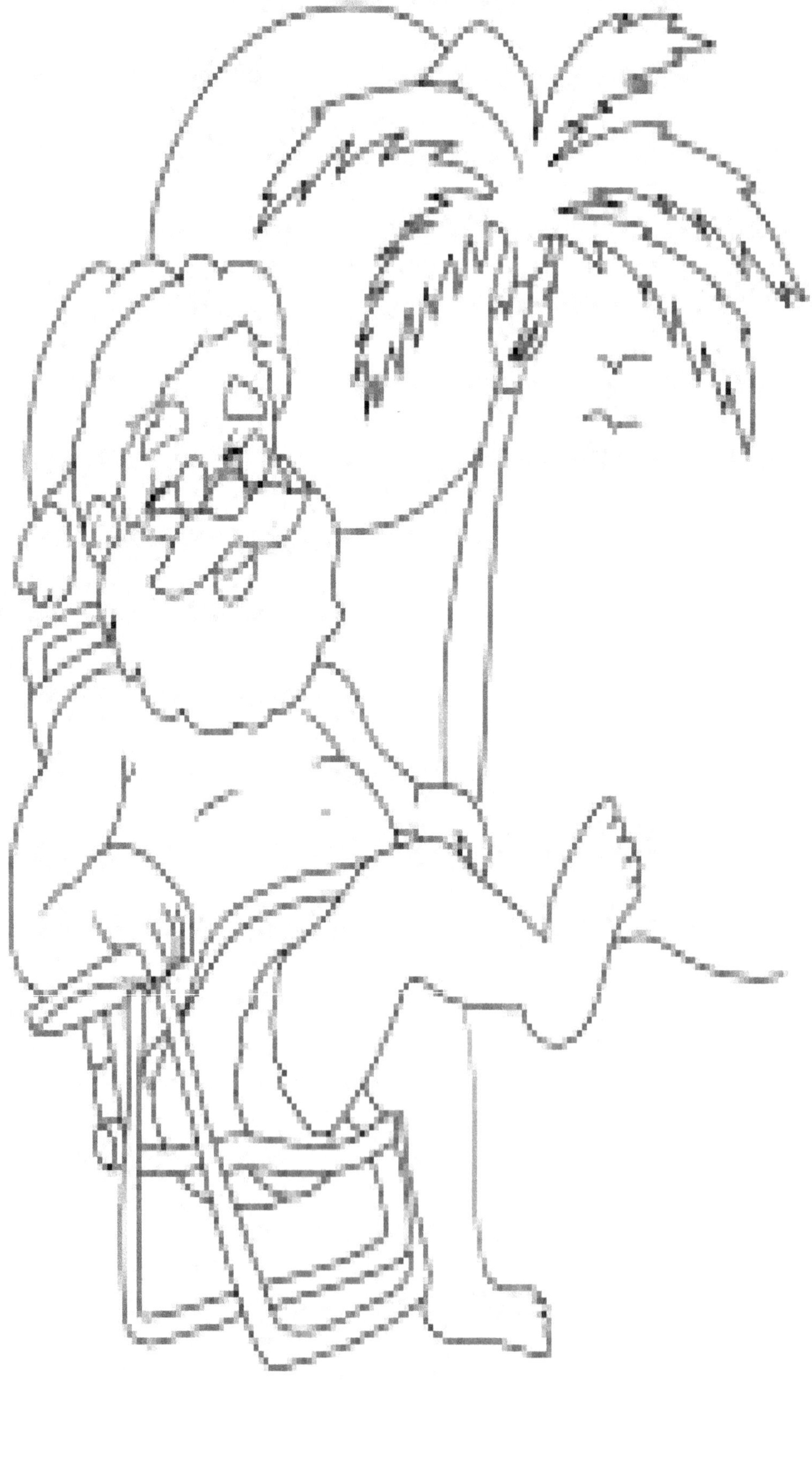

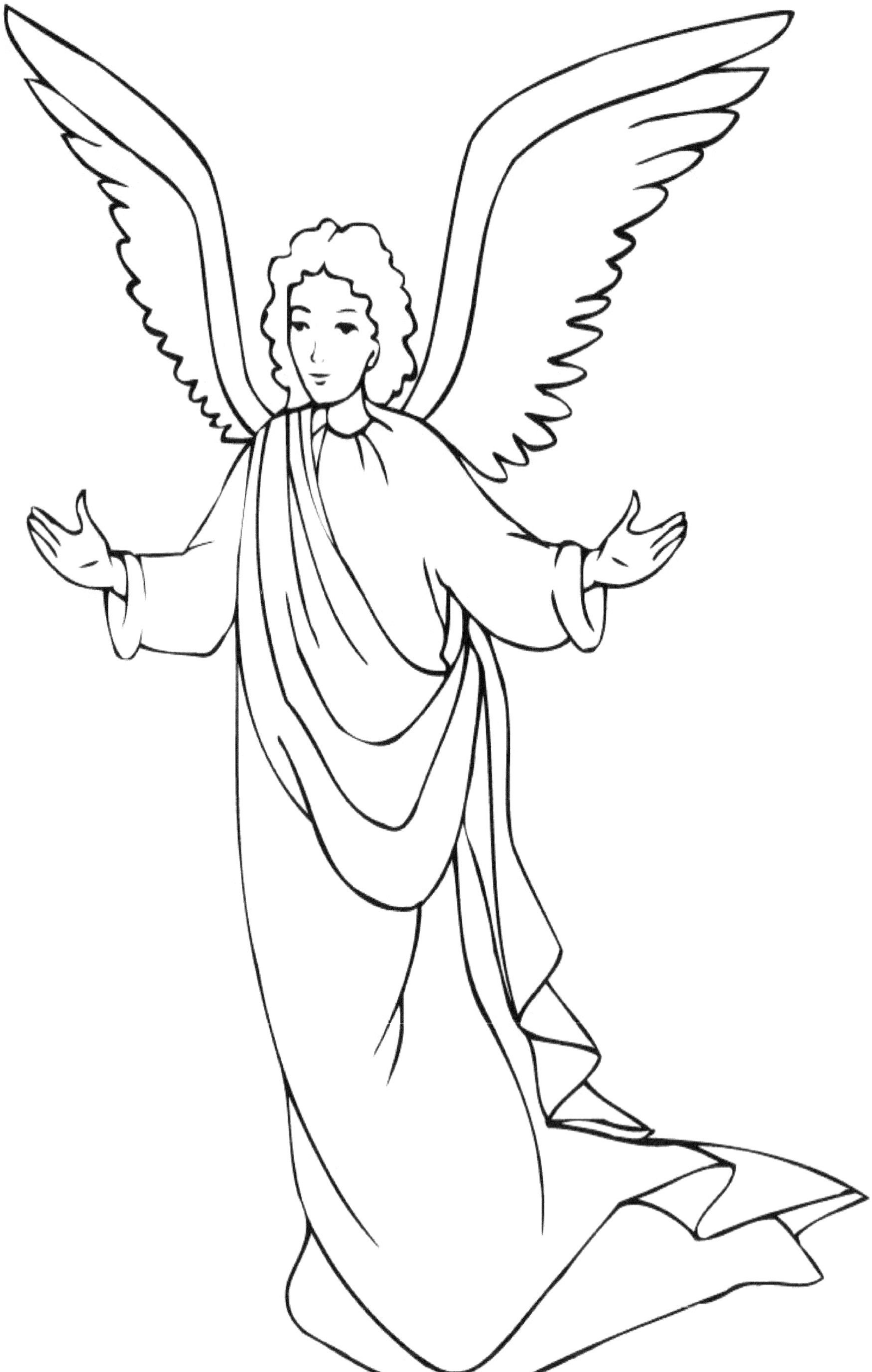

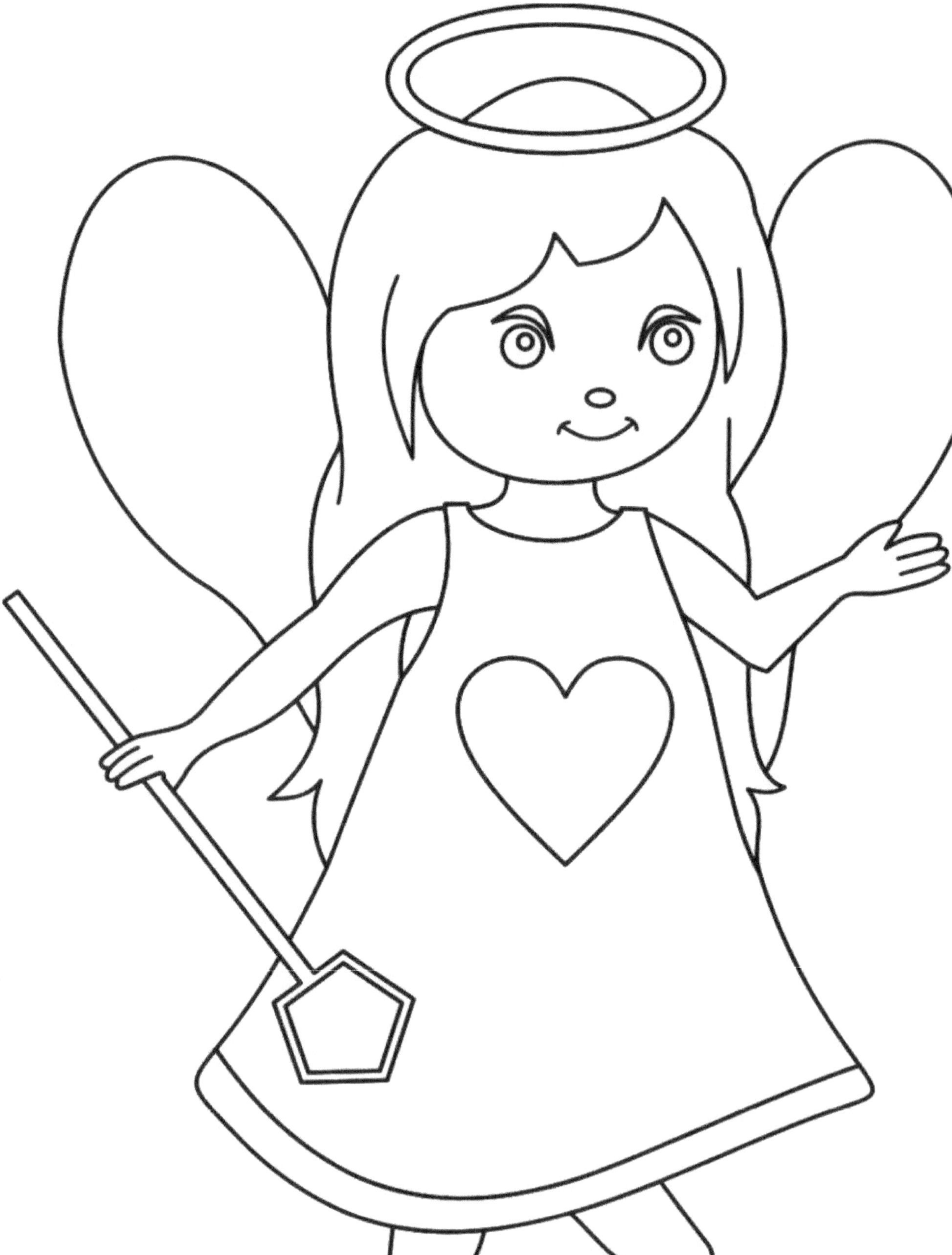

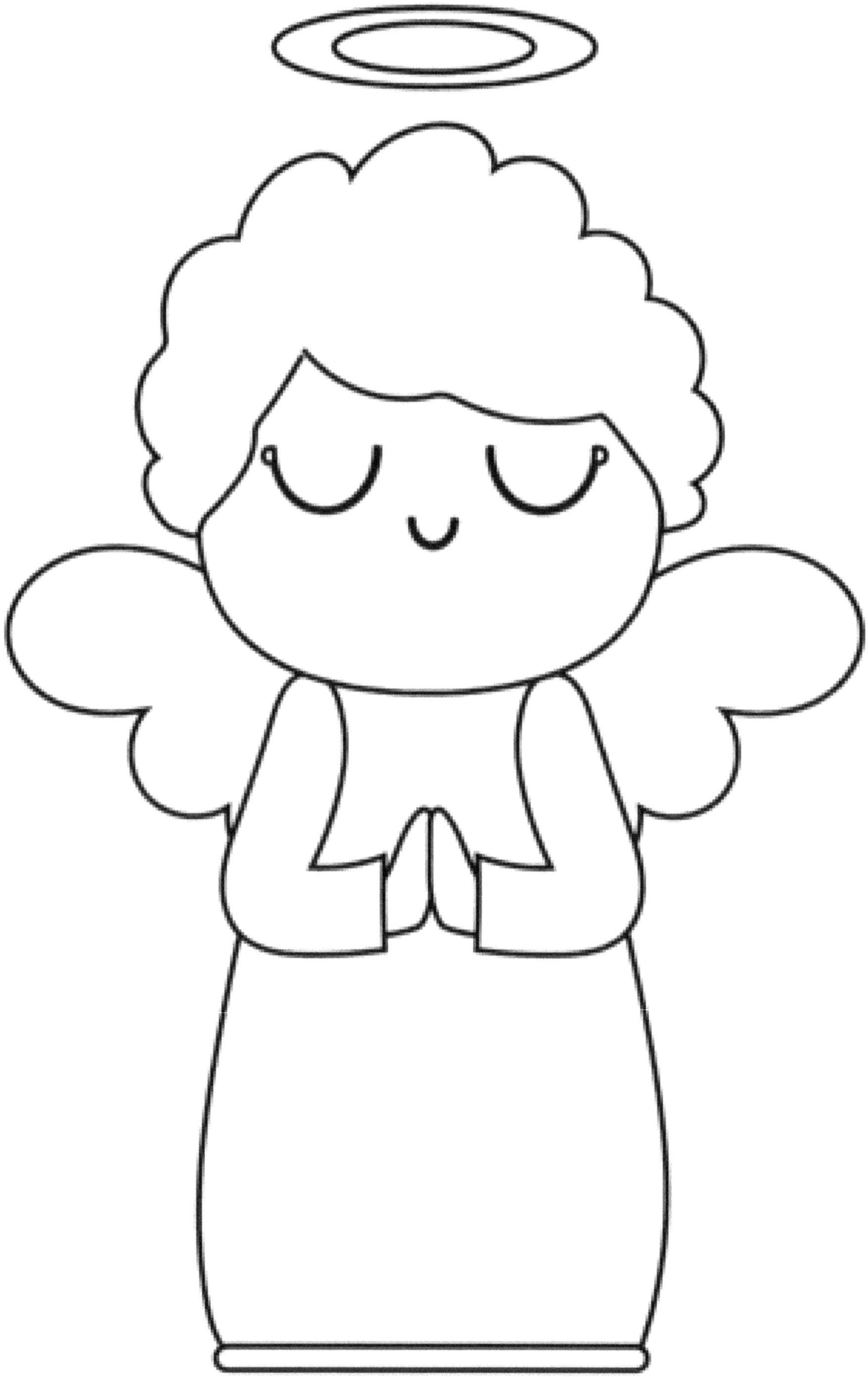

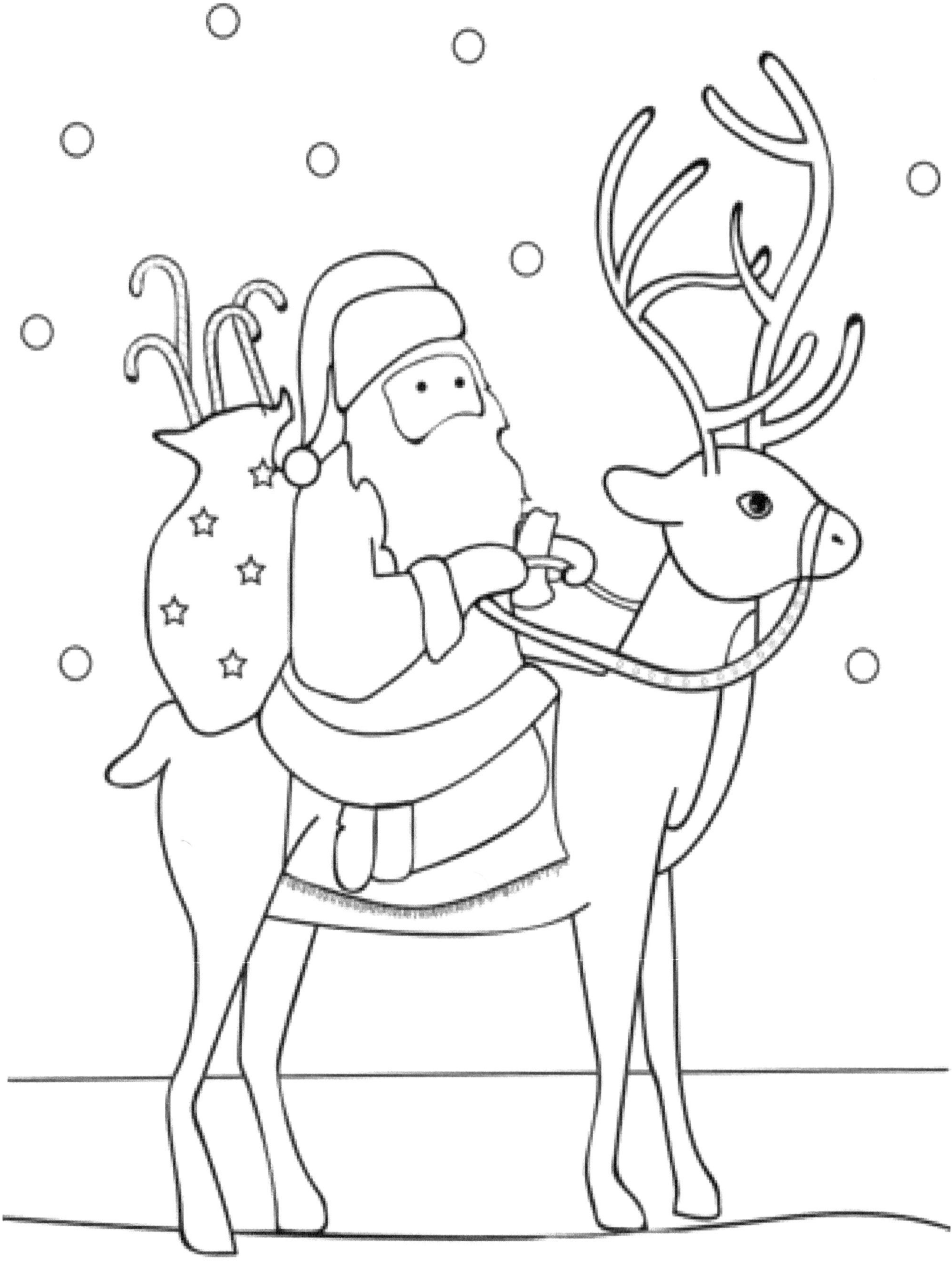

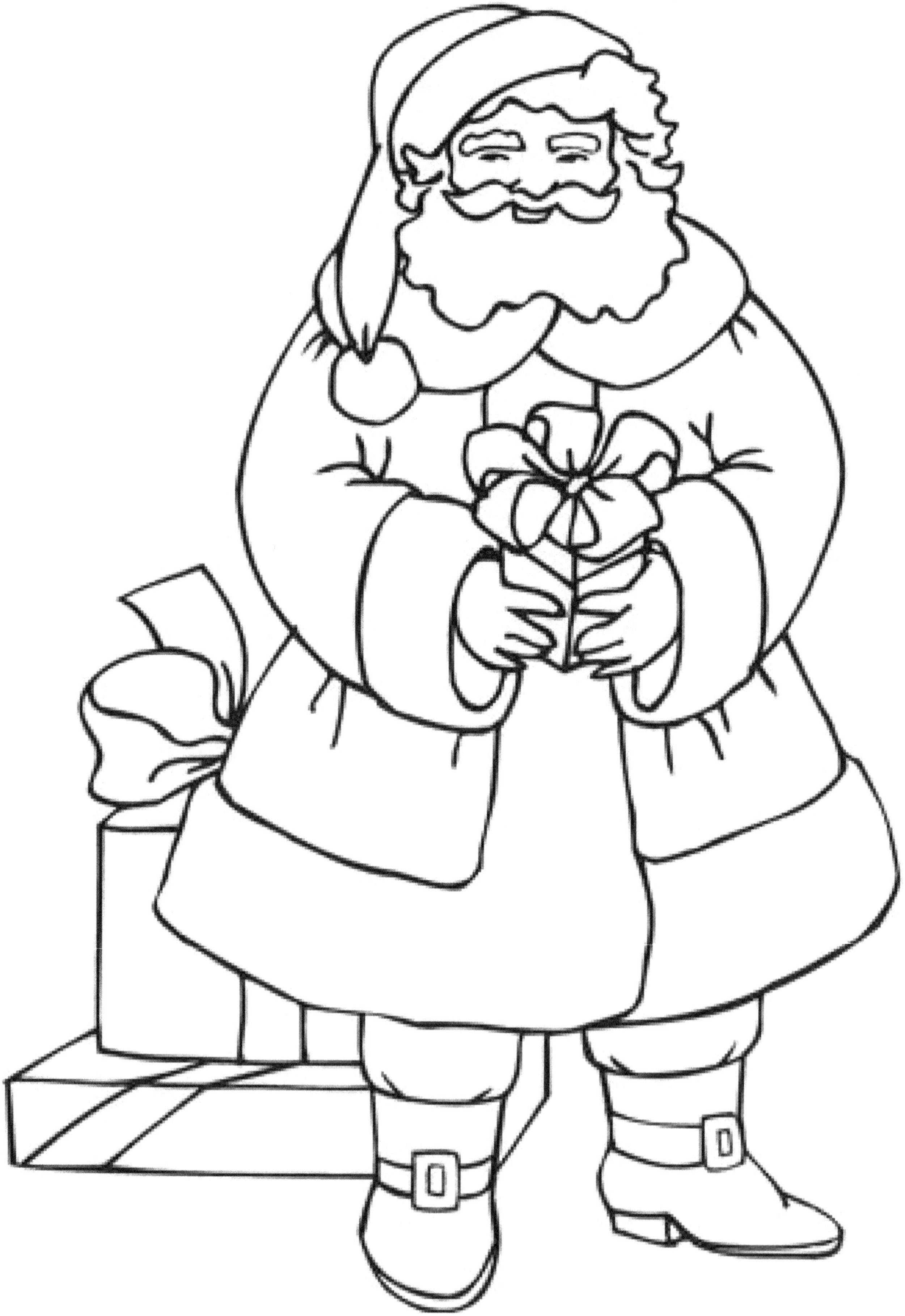

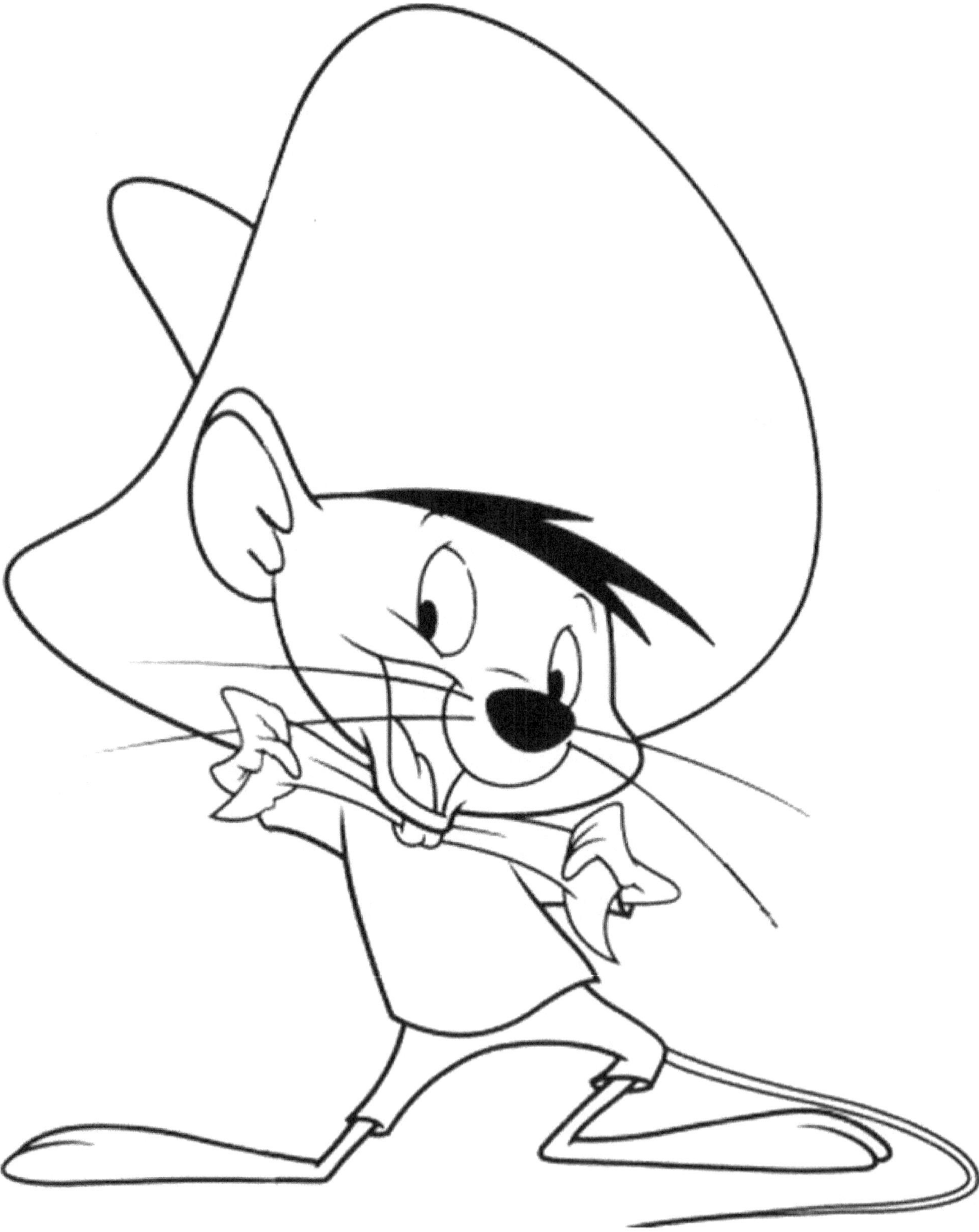

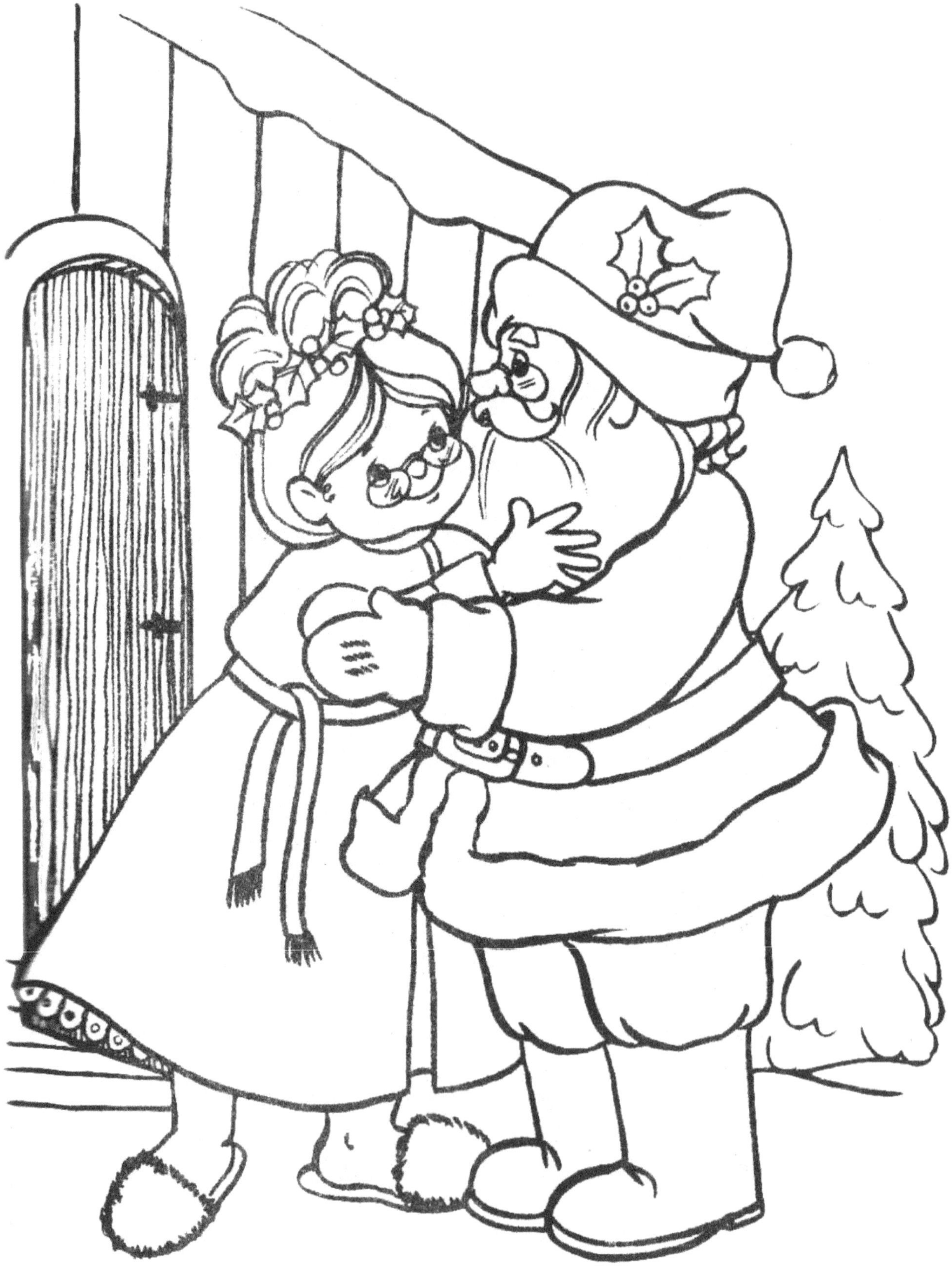

Printed in the USA
CPSIA information can be obtained
at www.ICGtesting.com
LVHW082251191124
797115LV00043B/1755
* 9 7 9 8 5 6 8 7 5 1 3 6 6 *